Library of
Davidson College

ERITREA and the UNITED NATIONS
and other essays

BEREKET HABTE SELASSIE

 **The Red Sea Press, Inc.**
Publishers & Distributors of Third World Books
556 Bellevue Avenue
Trenton, New Jersey 08618

The Red Sea Press, Inc.
556 Bellevue Avenue
Trenton, New Jersey 08618

First Printing 1989

Copyright © Bereket Habte Selassie

All rights reserved. No part of this publication may be reproduced, stored in a retrieval system or transmitted in any form or by any means electronic, mechanical, photocopying, recording or otherwise without the prior written permission of the publisher.

Typeset by TypeHouse of Pennington, Inc.

Cover design by Ife Nii-Owoo

Library of Congress Catalog Card Number: 88-62965

ISBN: 0-932415-12-1   Cloth

Contents

Acknowledgement ix

Preface xi

Chapter 1
International Legal Order Then and Now 1

Chapter 2
Eritrea and the United Nations 27

Chapter 3
Evolution of the Principle of Self-Determination 57

Chapter 4
The Law of Self-Determination and the Eritrean Case 73

Chapter 5
The American Dilemma on the Horn 99

Chapter 6
The World Bank: Power and Responsibility in Historical Perspective 123

Chapter 7
The Eritrean War and Prospects for Peace in the Horn of Africa 143

Chapter 8
Conclusion 157

Index 165

Dedication

To the heroic people of Eritrea who, in struggle, have lived the counsel of a great statesman, practicing defiance in adversity and magnanimity in triumph.

Acknowledgement

Several friends and colleagues have read parts of this volume of essays, each according to his/her areas of interest. Special thanks are due to professors Goler Butcher, Graham Hughes, David Mellinkoff, Immanuel Wallerstein, and to Michael Dow, Bill Ewing and Woldai Futur. The volume has benefited from their comments and criticisms, but needless to say I bear responsibility for any deficiency.

I am also thankful to Jean Paul Paddack for his research assistance, and to Julia Sweig, Ricky Bluthental and Sasha Natapoff for proof reading the final manuscript.

Some of these essays appeared in previous publications, and the publishers' permission to include them in the present volume is appreciated.

I also wish to record my gratitude to my university for the scholarly opportunities accorded me in the form of sabbatical leave. I wish especially to thank Dr. Robert Cummings and Dr. Sulayman Nyang, former and current directors respectively, of the African Studies and Research Program, and Dr. Michael Winston, vice president for Academic Affairs of Howard University. They have been unfailingly courteous and helpful to me for which I am most grateful.

Most important of all, I am grateful to my family, who bore my frequent absences with fortitude and quietly supported me. It is an expression of love which is its own explanation but which I never take for granted. It has sustained me in all my difficult moments.

Bereket Habte Selassie
Washington, D.C.

Preface

Bereket Habte Selassie is a scholar of many parts. He is at once a distinguished political scientist, a fervent nationalist and patriot, a spokesman for the anguish of his native land of Eritrea, and a cosmopolitan intellectual, fluent in a half dozen languages, equally at home in the corridors of the United Nations, the international academic conference, the third world political assembly, and the Eritrean *maquis*. The many facets of his brilliant career, and the diversity of his experience, leave their imprint upon this important book.

The dual themes of the volume are prefigured in the title: *Eritrea and the United Nations*. Bereket Selassie provides the historical context to the crystallization of "Eritrea" as a national idea, recounts the dreary narrative of diplomatic duplicity and Ethiopian imperial chauvinism which led to its 1952 incorporation in the patrimonial domain of Haile Selassie, and describes the birth and growth of the armed struggle for national liberation which followed ineluctably. To this political analysis is joined the jurisprudence of self-determination, and its application to the Eritrean case.

The combination of these two themes in one slender volume necessarily involves compression of treatment. For the full details of some aspects the reader may wish to complement this study with other important recent works. On the details of the evolution of the Eritrean liberation movements, their factional conflicts, and the consolidation of the Eritrean Peoples Liberation Front (EPLF) as the ascendant insurgent force, Markakis supplies invaluable supplementary data.[1] The international law of self-determination is given extended treatment and summation by Bucheit.[2]

Naturally, a book which marries scholarship and nationalism is not a monograph composed from the olympian heights of academic detachment. Bereket Selassie is an active participant in the EPLF, and a regular visitor to the combat zones. Liberation struggle is not an arid abstraction, but a passionate commitment. The vector of praxis necessarily permeates the pages of this work.

From this perspective, "the gap between the felt legitimacy of the Eritrean case for self-determination, and its poor reception in global diplomacy is a painful irony. In part, this reflects the chasm between the normative and empirical force of international law, a subject explored by the author with impressive erudition." Some might lay greater stress than does this text on the normative force of the regional international law created within the African diplomatic arena, particularly through the Organization of African Unity (OAU). The sanctification of the disputable doctrine of the *uti possedltis* by the 1964 OAU Summit at Cairo, deepening the commitment to extant frontiers enunciated in the 1963 founding Charter of the OAU, permitted Ethiopia to secure African judicial cover for its Eritrean annexation. The growing tendency of international law to defer to regional covenants is a major deterrent to Eritrean diplomacy in seeking legally-grounded external support.

There remains the realm of diplomacy per se, combined with an organized appeal to public opinion in the world at large. Here the Eritrean liberation movement has enjoyed far less success than the moral force of its self-determination claims might suggest, or that the extraordinary tenacity, perseverance, and heroism of its guerrilla struggle might justify. Partly, as Bereket Selassie well demonstrates, this reflects the effectiveness of Ethiopian diplomacy in representing the Eritrean struggle as mere "secessionism". The contrast, for example, in African state response to the claims of Polisario in the Western Sahara, recognized as a member state by the OAU, and the refusal to acknowledge the legitimacy of Eritrean self-determination claims, despite the obvious parallels between the juridical underpinnings of the arguments, is striking. If the remarkable diplomatic skills of the imperial state, under Menelik and Haile Selassie, had been matched by developmental effectiveness, perhaps Ethiopia would not be the famine-ridden land we know today.

In the politics of global diplomacy, most will agree with the author in his conclusion that both super-powers have subordinated their Horn policy to cold war strategic *raison d'etat*. The United States, the dominant external player from the end of World War II until the 1970s, placed priority on securing access to the Kagnew communications base (until it became obsolete in the mid-70s), and maintaining the security relationship with Haile Selassie established in the early 1950s. When the military dictatorship which succeeded the imperial regime invoked revolutionary socialist discourse as legitimating medium, and sought military banking to crush the Eritrean uprising as well as rebellion in many parts of the non-Amharic periphery, the Soviet Union provided massive support for the militarization and Leninization of the Ethiopian state. Although the USSR had opposed the initial 1952 annexation of Eritrea, in contemporary diplomacy both super-powers have essentially underwritten the Ethiopian position that "secessionism" rather than "self-determination" is at issue.

However, the guerrilla struggle is now more than a quarter-century old. For a second generation of Eritreans, armed combat has become a way of life. Even the five-fold increase in the size of the Ethiopian army, several billion dollars of heavy equipment, and Soviet direct logistical support have not permitted Addis Ababa to gain the upper hand; on the contrary, in March 1988 the Ethiopian army suffered its most humiliating defeat yet. But neither does the EPLF have the armed strength to achieve complete triumph on the battlefield.

Thus the tragic impasse so effectively illuminated in this book remains. Like [as] in such other prolonged struggles involving combat against an alien occupant as Algeria, Vietnam, Afghanistan, and Mozambique, ultimately peace can only come through a negotiated settlement. This can only be achieved through terms that those who have struggled against heavy odds and at incredible sacrifice can accept. There are indications that the changing texture of global international relations may be growing more favorable for a settlement; in 1988, several perennial conflicts moved toward resolution. "But such a happy outcome lies concealed beyond the horizon in the Eritrean instance. All those who peruse this volume better understand the reasons why."

Crawford Young
University of Wisconsin-Madison
September 1988

NOTES

1. John Markakis, "The Nationalist Revolution in Eritrea," *Journal of Modern African Studies*, XXVL, 4 (1988), pp. 51-70.
2. Lee C. Bucheit, *Secession: The Legitimacy of Self-Determination* (New Haven: Yale University Press, 1978).

Chapter 1
International Legal Order Then and Now

CONQUEST AND CONCORD

The history of international law is the history of the development of principles establishing rights and obligations, or imposing restraint among nations. International law has been honored more in its breach than in its observance, of course, as stronger states conquered or otherwise imposed their will upon weaker states, making and breaking treaties to suit their immediate aims or interests.

Nonetheless treaty rights and obligations have existed since ancient times, though not to the same extent nor with such degree of precision as is contained in modern treaties. Historically, the idea of formulating treaties emerged either from the need of weaker communities to combine their forces against a stronger power or, following conquest, as an imposition of the will of a conquering state. In the latter instance, the "peace treaty" expressed a new distribution of power, giving rise to a new condition of "normalcy." It was the functional equivalent to legislation and constitutional revision enacted by the legitimate authorities of a domestic government. It provided "a way for the community to adapt its organic law to new needs and energies that press for fulfillment."[1] It was the basis for a new legal order.

Pax Romana expressed the reality of the imperial Roman rule, following conquest. Pax Britanica referred to British control over a large portion of the world at the height of the British Empire, before the Second World

War. Pax Americana and Pax Sovietica also are used in a similar vein as terms referring to the spheres of influence or areas of control of the United States and the Soviet Union, respectively.

And more recently, a more ominous term—Pax Atomica—has been used as a function of the development of the frightful weapon of destruction, which imposes mutual restraint on those powers possessing it, out of fear of nuclear holocaust. At the same time, there is a degree of tolerance—even instigation in a number of cases—of local or regional wars which directly or indirectly advance the national interest of one or the other of the superpowers.[2]

Imperial expansion, in some sense, is as old as the human race, or at least as old as its social organization.[3] The extension of power of one's own group or the victory of one's side over others, does not need explanation as a human phenomenon. What does call for an explanation when it occurs in history is the *rejection* of opportunities for the extension of power, or the insistence on placing restriction on it. Whether because of expediency, or morality, or both, such restraint reflects sophistication, "overcoming the deep-seated urge for domination and power."[4]

As a general rule, military force has been used throughout history as a primary instrument of imperial policy. The Roman Legions were at once the direct expression of Roman power and the instrument of the defense and promotion of its imperial interest. But at the same time, the limit to military might was recognized. Out of expediency (recognition of the limits of power) mixed with the conviction that leaving the conquered peoples (at least some, like the Greeks) with optimum freedom as a worthwhile end in itself, the Romans extended the ideas of international legal order. Policy in Rome was determined by a governing oligarchy, whose attitudes to questions of conquest and restraint were sophisticated. During the second century B.C., such sophistication was characterized by avoidance of annexation of territories, from Carthage to Macedonia, despite strong pressure from some senators to annexation.[5]

But when rival powers achieved prominence, posing a threat to the Imperium, Rome would wage war and humble the aspirant as it did, for example, to Macedonia which was broken up into its four traditional constituent districts, made into separate "free" states. The overriding aim remained avoidance of annexation, which in terms of military power could have easily been done. Methods changed from leaving two or three regional powers to keep order, to fragmenting them when they became too powerful or ambitious.[6]

Yet, clearly, it cannot be said that the Roman oligarchy, albeit a sophisticated one, felt a moral repugnance towards aggression and domination or believed in the coexistence of equal and fully sovereign states. "Non-annexation, in fact, never meant non-intervention."[7] Rome was squeamish or "sophisticated" toward what it considered the civilized world, including Greece and Carthage. But beyond that, in a "Barbarian" fringe such as Spain, annexation was never questioned.[8]

And even within the "civilized" areas, such as Greece and Carthage, although independent states were staked and encouraged to exist in what Rome considered essential—their foreign policy—they were effectively under Roman control.

This historical pattern, epitomized by Roman policy, of distinguishing between (civilized) areas to be subject to "hegemonial" control and others ("barbarian") to be annexed continued to our own era in colonial history. The European colonial laws, like Roman law in earlier days, stood at the summit of the legal order with local laws accorded their rightful place, governing the lives of the majority of the conquered peoples. The Jus Gentium recognized under Roman law was the ancient equivalent of what colonial law referred to as "native" law in Africa.

The recognition of the laws of other peoples, even conquered peoples, with the supremacy of the law of the occupying power prevailing over certain areas of vital interest, is at the root of international legal order. Trade and mercantile commerce in later European history, particularly after the discovery of gold and silver, gave an impetus to the development of international law. European history from about 1500 to the end of the colonial era provides the most fertile ground for the genesis of "modern" international law. During the fifteenth century, the major powers of the period (Spain, France, and England) were—when not preoccupied with fighting each other—scenes of internal power struggles and territorial consolidation. The eventual outcome in each case was a stronger and more effective monarchical government.[10] It is not accidental that the concept of sovereignty, which will be discussed below, emerged in association with the consolidation of a centralized state with the monarchy as its core institution. An effectively organized state was often tempted with foreign adventures in search of more territory or revenue. Competing monarchies would vie with each other in this process, sometimes fighting wars, and making and breaking treaties.

Interstate warfare was punctuated by periods of peace and diplomacy. Peace-time relationship led to the belief that the state's natural tendency toward competition was not always best served on the battleground, and that security, aggrandizement, and the state's lesser goals might be gained through continuous peaceful liaison between governments. The practice of sending ambassadors on a permanent basis was an innovation which the city-states of Italy contributed to diplomacy during this period.[11]

There had already been some useful antecedent for the practice. Most states, as circumstances and resources allowed, kept secret agents in other countries, and commercial and banking firms maintained agents abroad, who also served as eyes and ears for the home government. Florence, under the Medicis, and Venice excelled in this practice.[12]

But the practice of maintaining permanent ambassadors began forty years after the Peace of Lodi n 1554, during which the permanent, regular diplomatic network became the principal channel of interstate relations, increasingly used for the settlement of territorial disputes, the negotiation of shifiting alliances, etc.[13]

Alongside the development of the institutions and procedures of diplomacy, the development of international law was part of Western European history in this period and thereafter. The jurisprudence of diplomacy was dominated by Western European scholars and statesmen. Of these, none has contributed more than the Dutch jurist, Grotius, who first explained the doctrine of *pacta sunt servanda* (obligations must be met) with clarity and vision, reflecting the era of mercantile capital. The three principal stages of capitalist development—merchant (or mercantile) capital, industrial capital, and finance capital—have seen corresponding stages of development of the colonial (imperial) system.[14].

Merchant capital initiated and dominated the first period of large-scale, overseas colonial expansion, marked by the "Merchant Adventures" plundering expeditions, slave trade, the establishment of trading stations, privileged monopoly trading companies, the conquest of newly discovered overseas territories, decimation of indigenous inhabitants, and establishment of colonial settlements by migration.[15]

Industrial capital was built on merchant capital, which was built on the "old colonial" system. Britain became the workshop of the world after the Industrial Revolution of the late 18th and early 19th centuries; raw materials were drawn from all over the world and British manufactured products dominated the world market; British shipping, under the protection of the British Navy, dominated world trade.

A new phase of the colonial system now emerged, repeating historic patterns of discrimination between two segments of people. On the one hand, in those territories such as Canada and Australia where settlers from Britain had established themselves on the basis of the decimation of indigenous inhabitants; these now developed as offshoots of, and subsidiary to, the ascendant British manufacturing class, supplying raw materials and receiving British manufactured goods. On the other hand, in the conquered territories such as India, the West Indies, and later Africa, where the British appeared as alien rulers and traders, the old colonial system (of tribute and exploitation) continued. The influx of British manufactured goods in these territories spread ruin among the native handicraft industries.

The superior economic power of Great Britain found its expression in the doctrine of *laissez-faire* and free trade. Where resistance occurred to this new "international law," warships and guns were employed to batter a way into these markets. The most notorious example of this ws the Opium War with China, conducted in the name of the right of the East India Company to force opium on the Chinese. At the conclusion of the first Opium War of 1840, the British extracted from the Chinese authorities as punishment for their resistance, the cession of Hong Kong. The legal right arising from the cession was thus based on a murderous war whose cause (*causus belli*) was one of the most reprehensible in history.[16]

During the last quarter of the 19th century, Britain lost industrial supremacy, first to the United States, and then to Germany. In 1880, British steel output stood at 1.3 million tons, American at 1.2 million, and German at 700,000 tons. By 1900, American steel output had reached 10.2 million, German 6.4 million and British 4.9 million tons. By 1913 this reached 31.3 million (American), 18.9 million (German) and 7.7 million (British) tons. But Britain still maintained first place in the export of manufactured goods, but with a decreasing portion.[17]

Britain still led the way in the areas of capital export and colonial expansion in this, the era of finance capital. The Berlin Treaty of 1884-85, which carved Africa into the colonial spheres of influence, represents the basis of a new legal order to the Africans in that the foundation for the state system they inherited after the end of the colonial era was laid by that Treaty.

INTERNATIONAL LAW IN THE ERA OF DECOLONIZATION

In terms of its content and major aims, international law has expressed the interests and power relationships of the major European powers, later joined by those of the United States of America. In short, traditional international law has been Euro-centric, serving the interests of European powers to the detriment and in utter disregard of much of the rest of the world, particularly the colonized world. But several developments in the twentieth century, and more particularly after the end of the Second World War, have led to the gradual reorientation of international law.

Of these developments, the Bolshevik Revolution of 1917 and the rise of the Soviet Union to the position of a major world power was the most important. No amount of protestation or denial, nor the behavior of the Soviet state in recent years, can alter the truth and the significance of this historical fact. The other developments are: the decline of the European colonial powers and the rise of the United States to step into their shoes as an economic and military superpower and, last but not least, the emergence of the former colonial peoples from dependence to independence.

The rise of the Soviet Union as a world power challenged the monopoly of Euro–American power in several respects. First, it became a major source of support to the colonial peoples. Second, the alternative vision of society that it presented in place of capitalism was a source of inspiration to thinkers and leaders of those territories, liberating them from the mental (intellectual) burden of an imposed history and an ideology born in the schools of the European metropoles. Third, and more relevant to the present discussion, as Soviet jurists would argue, its impact on the nature and direction of international law is unmistakable.[18]

Soviet jurists and statesmen contend that the evolution of international law in modern times is marked by its increasing "*democratization*," and its preeminent aim of peace among nations as the basis of sovereign equality. This is a juristic application of the democratic ideal as the most fundmental political principle of the modern era, the equality and self-determination of nations. As Bobrov observes, an "indispensable condition for the preservation of international peace and security . . . is free self-determination of all peoples," for which the Soviet Union fought resolutely in the Council of Nations until it became a generally accepted and universally applicable principle.[19]

Enlarging on the democratic content of contemporary international law and quoting other Soviet authorities, Bobrov notes that the principle of the sovereign equality of states extends not only to independent states, "but to nations fighting for their self-determination. The UN Charter elevates this principle to the status of law, and provides a profoundly democratic basis for the principle of the equality of states."[20]

The mandate of the United Nations and its historical agenda of decolonization is based on the charter. Its paramount principles, stated as "the purposes and principles" of the charter are,: maintenance of international peace and security[21] and fostering friendly relations among nations "based on respect for the principle of equal rights and self-determination of peoples."[22] In addition to these objectives the Charter adds a further basic purpose: "to achieve international cooperation in solving problems of an economic, social, cultural, or humanitarian character, and in promoting and encouraging respect for human rights and for fundamental freedoms for all without distinction as to race, sex, language, or religion."[23] Finally, the charter enjoins the United Nations to be "a centre for harmonizing the actions of nations in the attainment of these common ends."[24]

It should be recalled that the charter was adopted in the aftermath of a catastrophic war, with the sound of gunfire still ringing in the ears of most of those assembled at San Francisco. It is therefore perfectly understandable that the charter sought to build a new international legal order based on the principles summarized above. That the world community was considerably chastened by the horrors of war can be sensed from the stirring words of the preamble:

> We the people of the United Nations, determined to save succeeding generations from the scourge of war, which twice in our life time has brought untold suffering to mankind... and to establish conditions under which justice and respect for the obligations arising from treaties and other sources of international law can be maintained, and to promote social progress, and better standards of life in larger freedom... etc.

One of the lessons learned from the Nazi experience was the ease with which a group, one that considered itself and its "historic mission" above the law, flouted law and universally accepted standards of decency. The Nazis broke treaty obligations in violation of which they waged wars of aggression and invaded sovereign states.[25] Germany was a signatory to the Kellogg-Briand Pact, and the Nazi leaders were prosecuted partly for violation of the terms of that treaty, even with respect to crimes committed against countries that were not signatories, such as Denmark and Greece.[26]

The Kellogg-Briand Pact symbolizes the beginning of a shift towards a new development in international law, in that a group of nations entered into a compact renouncing war as a means of settling disputes, and "as an instrument of national policy."[27] And the Nuremberg trials marked the beginning of a new era. The war had also precipitated the end of the colonial era; the colonial/imperial idea was already discredited and stood on the defensive during the interwar years (1918-1939). After 1945 decolonization became inevitable. The question from then on was one of timetables and the "tutelage" of future governments.

The colonial powers attempted to use the idea of tutelage (colonial people are not ready for self-government) as a delaying tactic.[28] To this, the answer given by the movements for independence throughout the colonial world was "freedom now." The first phase of the decolonization process (1945--1960) is marked by such clamor for independence, vigorously backed by the Soviet Union, on the one hand; and the resistance of the former colonial powers on the other, with the United States standing inbetween, in benign ambiguity.[29]

The second phase of decolonization starts in 1960, when the pace quickened and the floodgate of independence was thrown wide open in Africa. The "Lancaster House Syndrome," synonymous with controlled change, takes over, under which the post-independence constitutions were drafted by the British colonial office and negotiated (at Lancaster

House in London) with the future African leaders. The French adopted a similar tactic under different procedures. Charles DeGaul decided to end the Algerian war. And in 1958, he offered independence to the rest of the African colonial empire under a French mini-international commonwealth called the "Communnaute."[30] "Meanwhile, the British Empire had been renamed the British Commonwealth, to which all former colonies and dominions could belong."[31]

The negotiated constitutional instruments reflecting principles of constitutional and international law, consecrated in the UN Charter and in the Universal Declaration of Human Rights of 1948, became integral parts of the emerging international legal order. The first such post-1945 constitutional instrument was that under which the Indian subcontinent (including Pakistan, before it split from India) achieved independence, which set a pattern for the later "independence constitution." A word of explanation is therefore worthwhile.

The new government in India (and later in Pakistan and Burma) was established by a decision in London and drew its authority from a British Act of Parliament. There was a preliminary plan which laid down conditions for the attainment of independence, enabling the British government to maintain the best possible conditions for defending its interests in the future. These included matters of defense, trade, and aid. In the case of Burma, the "aid" was a crushing debt burden imposed by treaty.[32]

This pattern repeated itself in Africa even more effectively. The constitutional machinery put in place was backed by the continuation of a bureaucratic structure, the judiciary and the security forces without much change. The forces of law and order continued, with indigenous hands gradually replacing European, but following the same procedures and applying laws inherited from the colonial past.[33] The characteristic feature of the post-colonial governmental structure was continuity with the colonial past which reflected, at a deeper level, structural (economic) continuity.

Thus, two parallel historical processes have been at work in the era of decolonization: the first is the liberaton of colonial peoples with the United Nations providing the highest forum for legitimacy in the colonial peoples' demand for independence; the second is the resistance of the colonial powers, expressed in subtle forms of indirect power retained through the emerging legal order. A review of some of the records of the United Nations General Assembly illustrates the first. The General Assembly resolutions in the years 1945-1965 on the question of national self-determination reveals an interesting pattern in which the United States acts as the arbiter of the forces of colonial domination and of liberation. As the numerical balance shifts with more newly independent states voting in favor of self-determination, the Soviet Union gains over the United States. This is reflected in the number of resolutions passed concerning the principle of self-determination as a supreme normative principle of international law.[34]

As a Soviet jurist might put it, sovereignty had become "democratized." Indeed, Bobrov said precisely that and added that this happened, thanks to the "enormous growth of influence wielded in international affairs by the world socialist system."[35] He also considered national liberation as a defense against aggression, and a guarantee for peace.[36]

PROBLEMS OF INTERNATIONAL LAW

The basic problem of international law may be expressed in terms of the definition, scope, and more specifically in terms of the nature and limit of the sovereignty of states. It is therefore useful to probe a little deeper on the theoretical and practical aspects of the concept of sovereignty.

As noted earlier, the principle of national self-determination has enabled the emergence of scores of new states from dependent status. On the other hand, formerly powerful states, that grudgingly gave up their former dominant (colonial) status, have seen the decline of their power. There is a twofold legal implication in this process. On the one hand, the newly independent states, anxious to defend their newly acquired independence, have stressed the importance of sovereignty and territorial integrity. The problem attendant to this attitude, justifiable as it is, has involved the overconcentration of power and the erosion of democratic principles and institutions. At the same time, the United Nations Charter, the Universal Declaration of Human Rights, and other instruments of international law have imposed conditions (democracy, human rights, etc.) on the exercise of state sovereignty.

On the other hand, the structures inherited from the colonial past and an increasingly integrated world economic and financial system places additional (in fact, more fundamental) restrictions on any notion of "unfettered" exercise of state sovereignty. The dialectical process, in which states seek to exercise their sovereignty in full measure and external forces and international law principles operate to place restrictions on that exercise, constitutes the essence of the problem of international law in its dynamic sense.

At a more theoretical level, the question arises: how can a sovereign state agree to place limits on its sovereignty? If it does place such limits, as it does when it signs a treaty imposing obligations on it, does this not constitute a fundamental contradiction to the concept of sovereignty?

In order to explore this question further, an explanation of the term treaty will be helpful. A treaty is defined as "an agreement normally entered into by two or more states under general international law."[37] A treaty, like a contract, is a legal transaction by which the contracting parties intend to establish mutual obligations and rights.[38] And what is "general international law?" Kelsen writes:

> By concluding a treaty the contracting states apply a norm of customary international law—this rule *pacta sunt servanda* (treaties must be, or ought to be, observed, that is have binding force)—and at the same time create a norm of international law, the norm which presents itself as the treaty obligation of one or of all the contracting parties, and as the treaty right of the other or others... Thus the treaty has a law-*applying* and at the same time a law-*creating* character.[39]

A treaty has a law-applying character because every conclusion of a treaty is the application of the rule of general international law—*pacta sunt servanda*. It has a law-creating character because every treaty constitutes obligations and rights that, prior to the conclusion of the treaty, had not yet existed, obligations and rights which come into existence by the treaty.[40]

In a less circuitous and more concise way, the British jurist, Lord McNair, has expressed the same point as follows;

> In every uncodified legal system there are certain elementary and universally agreed principles for which it is almost impossible to find specific authority. In the common law of England and the United States of America, where can you find specific authority for the principle that a man must perform his contract? Yet almost every decision on a contract presupposes the existence of that principle. The same is true of international law. No government would decline to accept the principle *pacta sunt servanda* . . .[41]

Grigory Tunkin, the noted Soviet jurist, offers a definition (of international law) that attempts to incorporate the new developments discussed above. Tunkin writes:

> Contemporary general international law can be defined as the aggregate of norms which are created by agreement between states of different social systems, reflect the concordant wills of states and have a generally democratic character, regulate relations between

them in the process of struggle and cooperation in the direction of ensuring peace and peaceful coexistence and freedom and independence of peoples, and are secured, when necessary, by coercion effectuated by states individually or collectively.[42]

Tunkin's definition goes beyond a treaty, but is inclusive of a treaty. It is clear that the phrase "states of different social systems" is meant to indicate the coexistence of socialist and capitalist systems. But it implies that there may not be agreements between or among states with the same or similar social systems, which clearly could not have been the author's intention, for that would invalidate the Warsaw Pact, among others.[43]

The obligations that a treaty imposes on a state may thus also be imposed by "general international law." Tunkin's definition which marks an advance over traditional conceptions, nonetheless reflects a formal adherence to the traditional view. International law is becoming more and more complex and many-sided, as Friedmann has pointed out. The scope is expanding with the growth of the organization of mankind on universal and regional bases.[44] "Private law may become public law and a comparative study of [a] particular subject may become the prelude for an international convention."[45]

More generally, from the public viewpoint, it should be noted that there are contradictory attitudes regarding international law. On the one hand, there are the cynics who dismiss it as utterly useless; and on the other hand, there are the idealists who expect too much from it. As Brierly has reflected, there is "the practical man who imagines that he has shed his illusion" and "the ultra-legalistic lawyer who deals in codes and formulas as though they contained a magic of their own, or the enthusiastic layman who imagines that earnest aspirations after a better international order can take the place of patient study of the problem concerned."[46]

INTERNATIONAL OBLIGATION AND SOVEREIGNTY

Clearly, in the light of historical experience, humanity can ill-afford to dismiss international law as useless. It can also hardly afford to ignore its problems. There are two principal problems concerning the legal character of international law, with which legal theory has grappled. Both problems arise from the comparison of international law with municipal (national) law. An eminent legal theorist, H. L. A. Hart, has contended that the first problem is rooted in the conception of law "as fundamentally a matter of orders backed by threats, and in comparing international law with municipal law."[47] The second problem, which flows from the first, rests on the belief that states cannot by definition be subject of obligation.[48]

The principle of state sovereignty has been the cornerstone on which international relations has been built. And this principle has been clearly stated in, and reinforced by, the Charter of the United Nations.[49]

How then can a state be subject to international obligation? An allied question is that international law is said to be not binding because it lacks sanctions. Hart argues that this latter scepticism is less difficult theoretically because, "if one day international law were reinforced by a system of sanctions, the present objection [would be] based on a radical inconsistency, said or felt to exist, in the conception of a state which is at once sovereign and subject to law."[50] Hart then traces this serious question, as already noted, to its origin in municipal law, in which the concept of sovereignty is associated with the idea of a person above the law, whose word is law for inferiors or subjects.[51]

From the sixteenth century onwards, the symbolic identification of state and monarch no doubt nourished the idea. Hart considers it important for the understanding of international law "to shake off these associations." The expression, "a state," is not the name of some person or thing inherently or "by nature" outside the law; it is a way of referring to two facts: first "that a population inhabiting a territory lives under that form of ordered government provided by a legal system with its characteristic structure of legislature, courts and primary rules,[52] and second that the government enjoys a vaguely defined degree of independence."[53]

A more fruitful approach to Hart, would be to start with the idea of limits (or what he calls "negative force"). A sovereign state "is one *not* subject to certain types of control, and its sovereignty is that area of conduct in which it is autonomous." Some measure of autonomy is imparted by the very meaning of the word state, but the contention that this *must* be unlimited or *can only* be limited by certain types of obligations is not warranted.[54] Put in a comparative perspective, the question for municipal law is: What is the extent of the supreme legislative authority recognized in this system? For interntional law it is: What is the maximum area of autonomy which the rules allow to states?[55]

Hart also deals with the "voluntarist theories" or theories of "auto-limitation" which attempted to reconcile the (absolute) sovereignty of states with the existence of binding rules in international law by treating international obligations as self-imposed. Like their counterpart in political science—the social contract theory—these theories fail to explain, first, how it is known that states "*can*" only be bound by self-imposed obligations, in advance of any examination of the actual character of international law. Second, in order for a state to impose an obligation upon itself through a promise, an agreement, or a treaty, *rules* must already exist providing that a state is bound to meet its obligations. Such rules, presupposed in the very notion of a self-imposed obligation, obviously cannot derive their obligatory status from a self-imposed obligation to obey them.[56]

The logic of Hart's argument is irresistible and most illuminating of a highly problematic juristic/political concept. Such analysis is invaluable in helping to rescue universal concepts such as sovereignty from the *dead hand* of the past, and in reinterpreting their contemporary use more realistically. Logic alone is not enough of course in the life of the law; it has to be tempered with experience. And experience, particularly of the last half-century, has shown that the alternative to law is conflict; it is also an evolving concept and, as such, it should be part of the solutions to problems instead of being part of the problem.

Related to the theoretical problems summarized above, there are practical problems which must also be noted here. To begin with, in the hard school of experience, we learn that few of the newly independent nations attained their sovereign statehood without a bitter struggle. The concessions ultimately yielded to them by the former metropolitan powers were made only in answer, and in proportion, to the strength of the national revolt or demand. Only in the latter phase of decolonization did those powers readily accept demands for independence and, in all cases, the constitutional structures were designed to ensure continuity of interests, as we have seen. Diplomatic relations are established, obviously to maintain, protect, and advance interests.

Soviet writers never tire of reminding the Third World that the Soviet Union itself faced attempts on its sovereignty in its early years. As Bobrov contends, the Soviet Union and its jurists have supported respect for state sovereignty both on the grounds of principle and on their own experience in the 1920s.[57] Third World writers and statesmen have echoed these sentiments at times when their newly independent states were fragile and vulnerable to external pressures.[58]

Nor was this limited to Soviet writers or Third World statemen and writers. Joseph Kunz, writing as early as 1957 observed: "Despite all changes, it has not been possible to ban the spirit of sovereignty from international law."[59]

Sovereignty, then, is an established principle of international relations. But international relations is not about iron-clad principles, and international law is fundamentally based on a need for the orderly exchange of goods and services across national boundaries. The "sovereign flow" of commerce impinges on the political sovereignty of states, causing restraint, forbearance, or (even at times) sacrifice in return for the benefits of orderly conduct and predictability.

The assault on sovereignty has come from two different directions. The first is direct assault in the form of invasion or occupation. It would be interesting to know how Bobrov would explain the Soviet incursion into

Afghanistan in 1979 and the continued presence there of some 100,000 Soviet troops, for he had defended the principle of sovereignty in absolutist terms. He asserted that "there is no doubt that this principle will be increasingly important in the future, for there can be no progress in the development of peaceful coexistence of present day states if it is not strictly observed."[60]

There is no need to cite other examples of direct infringement of state sovereignty. But infringement has not come only in direct forms. A more insidious form of intervention in the domestic affairs of a sovereign state has come from sources other than states, contributing to the erosion of sovereignty in our time.

First, as collectivism replaced a *laissea-faire* approach in economic organization, a large number of questions have become subject to governmental regulation, where they transcended national boundaries.[61] Among the unintended consequences of this development is the increased importance accorded to treaties in international law which define and regulate the respective roles of states concerning such transnational questions.

Second, the development of modern technology and communication, and the expansion of trade have made states more "interdependent." Nowhere is this interdependence more dramatically illustrated than in the area of atomic science and technology. The accident in the nuclear reactor Chernobyl in the Ukraine and the shock waves it sent among peoples of neighboring countries serves as a poignant reminder of this reality. The common danger implicit in this kind of technological development, extending beyond national boundaries which define sovereign statehood, has introduced an element of artificiality into any rigid conception of sovereignty.

Finally, the rise of the multinational corporations with a monopoly over critical sectors of the economies of sovereign states has already partially altered the basis of traditional international relations. The multinational corporation is perhaps the most prominent international actor in the world today, crossing ideological and geographical boundaries, where the angels of officialdom would fear to tread.[62]

Increasing attention must therefore be paid to the role and power of multinational corporations and their impact on international relations, particularly in the developing countries where they have already carved out huge chunks of power, vying with the power of the state in the host countries. The political power of the state in African countries, for example, confronts daily the economic power of the multinational corporation in a process that has not only social and economic consequences, but legal implications as well.

The challenge of this powerful economic force which has broken out of the traditional mold (of the earlier joint stock company) involves crosscutting power in which a parent company registered in one country can determine policies across state boundaries through its ownership of economic interests in other states, overseen by interlocking directorates.[63] To the multinational corporation, the world is one vast opportunity, one unified field for investment, production, distribution, and exchange.

Driven by the profit motive, the multinational corporation has proven to be politically colorblind or, to vary the metaphor, a chameleon that can change color to accommodate to changing circumstances, in order to achieve its primary objective. In the process it has had an unmistakable impact on the political and social landscape in the countries where it operates.

Legal order is of great concern to the multinational corporation, as it requires a climate of stability and predictability to profit. This does not necessarily include human rights, as South Africa and Chile under Pinochet demonstrate, where multinationals have been doing business virtually unconcerned about the absence or grave violations of human rights.[64]

CONCORD OR CALAMITY

Nation states have a long way to go before they attain harmony. Contentious issues divide some and unite others. Considerations of reciprocity of interest, mutual benefit, and convenience, among other reasons, compel them to seek orderly conduct creating the conditions for international law in the first place. If the orderly exchange of goods and services among nations may be considered to be the foundation of international relations; in an increasingly interdependent world system, the law that stands behind that system, or that regulates such orderly exchange, or mediates between conflicts arising from it, would constitute the life-blood of the system.

Falk reminds us that "even in wartime the desire to avoid chaos by the maintenance of communication and by refraining from belligerent excess gives law the important task of generating mutually acceptable norms capable of clear discernment and adequate implementation."[65] In peacetime the orderly process continues in the assumption of the primacy of commonly held normative principles, in the expectation that promises will be kept, that *pacta sunt servanda*.

But divisive issues continue to dog international relations as they do within nations. The issues that divide national (domestic) communities are social, economic, and political. A national government is, however, normally able to mobilize normative and material resources to avoid the worst effects of conflicts, if not resolve them completely, at any rate. Within domestic communities (inside sovereign states), there is solidarity based on historically evolved or legislatively prescribed common normative standards. The history of civil rights legislation in the United States is a good example of this.

Much of the world is still beset with conflicts which spill across state boundaries and which, at times, invite foreign intervention. From the standpoint of the international legal order, a number of questions persist, demanding answers. The most important set of questions may be summed up by asking: When is intervention justifiable, taking us back to the vexing question of sovereignty. Many regional conflicts or conflicts within states, which have invited the intervention of one external power or another over the last twenty-five years, raise this question.

International law, which has achieved a degree of maturity in the development of normative principles applicable to the mediation of conflicts (both within and among states), has yet to evolve the institutional mechanisms for the effective application of those principles. The application of law within domestic societies is difficulty enough.[66] The difficulties of enforcing law within domestic communities that arouses communal hostility and civil strife are compounded in the international community where nations maintain "the dominant tradition that the simultaneous pursuit of national interest by the countries of the world presupposes patterns of conflict more than structures of cooperation."[67]

In a world that has supposedly become more "integrated," paradoxically conflicts persist in two basic areas which are related: ideological and economic.

On the Horns of a Dilemma

The misgivings expressed about international law, noted earlier, have been prompted by the absence of an international system of government— a world legislature, courts with compulsory jurisdiction and centrally organized enforcement bodies. But the theory and practice behind the *legality* of international law has been with us for well over a century and a half, and the existing usage stemming from such long experience cannot be dismissed. Rather, the principles that have guided it should be subject to continual scrutiny and clarification in a slowly evolving international order.[68]

The creation and growth of the United Nations has reinforced those principles, acting as "a centre for harmonizing the actions of nations in the attainment of (these) common ends."[69] The United Nation's failure to develop institutional mechanisms for the application of these principles reflects the central dilemma of international relations—and the sovereignty principle is at the heart of that dilemma. On the one hand, sovereignty occupies a paramount place in the international normative value system. On the other hand, many regimes [of "ill-repute"] use it in pursuit of unjust or oppressive domestic policies, and invoke it in defense against any form of intervention from outside.

To break out of this dilemma (or at the very least to attenuate its ill-effects), two sets of guarantees are required: (a) a system of guarantees that would ensure the "good behavior" of states, in accordance with prescribed standards with respect to a number of crucial issues, including human rights; and (b) a system of guarantees that would secure the sovereign independence of states, particularly those of the Third World.

As for the first, the United Nations itself has done a good job in fulfilling the requirements and laying down general principles, beginning with its charter and in several other legal instruments, including the Universal Declaration of Human Rights of 1948, numerous resolutions[70] and conventions.[71] The member states themselves—with a few exceptions, notably South Africa—have adopted the essential elements of those fundamental principles in their respective national constitutions. But many continue to engage in practices, flagrantly violative of some of the principles.[72]

The United Nations has been virtually helpless in redressing wrongs caused by such violations, or in causing changes in policies and practices. In explaining the United Nation's failure, it is important to remember that the organization is only a little more than the sum total of its parts—its members. And the majority of its members belong to blocs of states, many of whom could not possibly get a clean bill of health in the area of human rights. The United Nations is as much an agency for change as it is a reflection of the policies and politics of its member states.[73] It has at its disposal the normative resources which enable it to exert pressure, placing any violator on the defensive. It is these resources and their acceptance by the international community at large that make the United Nations more than the sum total of its parts. That margin of difference, though fragile, is of crucial value, and the inordinate growth of non-governmental organizations (NGOs) concerned largely with human rights and basic needs is a testimony to this value.[74] (This growth of NGO's may be explained, in part, as an aspect of the failure of the United Nations, exposing a need that must be filled by non-official bodies with a capacity to move faster and speak more freely. It is a response to the challenge posed by the dilemma surrounding sovereignty noted above.

As for the second set of guarantees—a system that would secure the sovereign independence of states—governments in the Third World seek to defend the integrity of their states from both iternal and external sources of danger, or potential danger. Internally, the "security imperative" seeks to minimize local division or conflict by insisting on national unity or integration. Expenditures for security forces have increased enormously as a result, and the financial as well as political implications of this imperative have been far reaching.[75] At the same time, the dominance of one-party governments, in many cases based on the dominance of one or two national (or ethnic) groups, in the political life of nations does not inspire confidence in the rhetoric of national unity. Instead of "integrating" diverse groups it tends to polarize politics, sometimes leading to rebellion. Paradoxically then, in a world that is becoming more "integrated," the need for diversity has become one of the guarantees of real harmony. People instinctively resort to local autonomy, of varying degrees, as a defense against the "unifying" or "mobilizing" propensity of the state—and indeed of American corporate capitalism or of Soviet "non-capitalist" development politics.

To reiterate the relevance of sovereignty as a problem, in a different way, it can act as a shield against external intervention, but also as a sword against internal demands which the state may find unacceptable, rightly or wrongly. The domestic national groups, on their part, resort to diversity as a weapon of defense or in pursuit of whta they consider to be legitimate group interests.[76] One of the intriguing political phenomena in recent years is the argument asserting the primacy of "class interest" as a defense against legitimate national (or ethnic) demands for autonomy. Ethiopia today is a prime example of the use or abuse of such arguments.[77]

At what point does the promotion of class struggle stop in the interest of general peace and welfare? What criteria exist to mediate between the conflicting demands of class and national (ethnic) interests, to the extent that they can be said to be based on legitimate grounds? Who decides on whether either is based on legitimate grounds?

These questions raise important issues of conflict of normative values not appropriately covered by the array of resolutions and other instruments of the United Nations or not covered in terms of the manner in which "class interest" has been advanced to defeat legitimate national interests.[78] The issue of class versus nationality or other social or political categories reflects larger issues of ideological division in the world characterized by the bipolarity of international relations in our times. The way in which the leaders of the Third World have sought to deal with that bipolarity, both in defense of sovereign independence and as a strategy to play a more autonomous role in world politics, has become a crucial part of international relations in our time.[79]

For some thirty years now a new political phenomenon has made its presence felt in international relations. It is known by the name "Non-

Alignment," and is closely linked with the post-war history of decolonization and the determination of the Third World states not to be engaged on the side of one or the other of the superpowers.

The continued dominance of the former colonial powers and the United States of America in their national economies, which perpetuated dependence and the political fragility of most of the newly independent states, impelled the leaders of some states to combine and assert their "neutrality" in the global contention of the superpowers. The Bandung meeting of 1955 institutionalized the process of periodic meetings and consultations, facilitating formation of blocs at the United Nations. As already noted, this development had the effect of eventually altering the balance of forces at the United Nations General Assembly in favor of the Soviet Union, which historically supported the independence of the Third World countries.[80] But there is no automatically operating Third World bloc support for any Soviet agenda at the United Nations. For one thing, several Third World countries are ideologically and geopolitically closer to the United States. Most are also economically linked with the United States and its Western allies. Morevoer, the United States, even under a conservative administration like Reagan's, has found the UN's good offices and political forum helpful in many instances. The recent UN mediation effort in Afghanistan is a good example.[81]

Third World countries have developed the concepts of "positive neutrality" and "non-alignment" to guide their international relations. The two concepts have been used interchangeably, with non-alignment gradually gaining currency. As originally conceived, five elements constituted the concept of non-alignment:

1. An independent policy based on peaceful coexistence;
2. Support of national liberation movements;
3. Non-involvement in collective military pacts;
4. Non-involvement in bilateral agreements with any of the superpowers; and
5. Refusal to grant military bases to foreign powers.

In this novel conception of international peace and cooperation, the world is no longer seen in the prism of bipolarity— of two opposed camps with the rest of the world tied to one or the other superpower. Nor is the interpretation given to the concept of peaceful coexistence by the superpowers necessarily shared by the adherents of non-alignment. One of the best exponents of this concept is the Algerian jurist and statesman, Mohamed Bedjaoui.[82] Bedjaoui explains the superpower conception of peaceful coexistence as a *modus vivendi* between East and West, without the least desire to realize universal models for establishing and developing relations among all states, irrespective of their differing political and social system.[83]

The non-aligned countries also stress their adherence to the principles of the United Nations Charter. And based on those principles and the profound desire of humanity for universal peace, they seek to stay away from any alliance with one or the other of the superpowers. They consider their policy a precondition for the preservation of their ideal of national independence. Indeed, they consider it a guarantee of world peace, by acting as a deterrent to the antagonism of the two big blocs.

Starting with the meeting in Belgrade in 1961, the non-aligned countries have made strenuous attempts to fulfill the aims expressed in the five elements of non-alignment listed above. In their support of national liberation movements, they used the resources of the United Nations effectively to speed up the process of decolonization. They also used their regional organizations such as the Organization of African Unity (OAU) to provide assistance to liberation movements and to draw world interest to their just struggle. In recent years, some of the remaining liberation movements, such as the Western Saharan and Eritrean movements have become divisive.[84]

The requirements of non-involvement in military pacts and non-participation in bilateral alliances with the superpowers, together with the imperative of peaceful coexistence, have also been regarded as crucial in the fulfillment of the objectives of non-alignment—universal peace and national independence. Military pacts often involve the building of foreign military bases. Any involvement in military pacts would nourish the spirit of the cold war and th arms race, and ultimately imperil both peace and the national sovereignty of small nations. The same holds for foreign military bases.

In all cases where "objective" historical conditions have forced states not to fulfill any of these requirements, all efforts are made to encourage them to reduce their dependence on foreign powers.[85] This raises the difficult question of continued dependence of many Third World countries on their former colonial rulers or on the United States and Japan for their economic survival. The non-alignment principle admits this reality. Rather than dogmatically insist that these countries "delink" immediately as a condition of membership of the non-aligned states, they try together to evolve a Third World strategy to transform the conditions that led to, and perpetuate, this dependence.

The emergence of UNCTAD (the United Nations Conference for Trade and Development) as a forum for airing and attempting to redress Third World grievances is part of this strategy.[86] This aspect of Third World struggle is perhaps the msot crucial aspect of non-alignment and, if successful, may well be the basis for a true international legal order. As such, it is an appropriate topic with which to conclude this discussion.

Any legal order, to be just, must be based on a just economic and social order. The present international economic order is based on an unequal relationship, historically conditioned and maintained by the international legal and financial order, epitomized in the Bretton Woods institutions. The attempts of the Third World countries to restructure the international economic order found legitimacy when the United Nations General Assembly passed a resolution accepting the Third World demand for a new international economic order (NIEO). But a NIEO remains a dream yet to be realized. The promise of the UN Charter to promote social progress and establish better living conditions "in a larger freedom" is a fundamental premise of peace and stability.[87] Legal order, imposed on peoples under conditions of inequality and injustice at any level (national, regional or international), has no guarantee of peace. In defeating the aims of a NIEO, the industrially advanced countries have only postponed (not resolved) the conflict inherent in the present international legal order. It is to be hoped that wiser counsels will prevail.

NOTES

1. Richard A. Falk, *Law, Morality and War in the Contemporary World* (New York: Praeger, 1983), p. 73.
2. US Secretary of Defense, Caspar Weinberger, opened a conference on "low intensity warfare" with this observation: "Tonight, one out of every four countries around the world is at war. In virtually every case, there is a mask on the face of war. Behind the mask is the Soviet Union and those who do its bidding." (*Washington Post*, April 27, 1986). Soviet spokesmen have traditionally charged that US imperialism is more widely and insidiously spread through quiet intervention in the affairs of other countries.
3. Cf. E. Badian, *Roman Imperialism in the Late Republic*, 2nd ed. (Ithaca, NY: Cornell University Press, 1981), p. 1.
4. Ibid.
5. Ibid.
6. Ibid.
7. Ibid.
8. See, for example, C.H.V. Sutherland, *The Romans in Spain 217 BC-AD117* (New York: Barnes and Noble, London: Methuen), 1939.
9. See Charles Carter, *The Western European Powers, 1500-1700* (Ithaca, NY: Cornell University Press, 1971), pp. 20-36.
10. Ibid.

11. Ibid.
12. Carter informs us that during the peaceful period between the sixteenth century wars of religion and the Thirty Years' War; Spain, the predominant power of Europe, increasingly depended on diplomacy. In a comparable period of French preponderance, Louis XIV maintained twenty-one permanent embassies. England, far more typically, kept only five embassies in the period 1660-1680, while sending diplomatic missions to a total of thirty separate rulers. See Charles Carter, op cit., p. 25. See also Phyllis S. Lachs, *The Diplomatic Corps Under Charles II and James II* (New Brunswick, NJ: Rutgers University Press, 1965), p. 4-5.
13. Carter, op. cit.
14. For a useful study on the impact of these three stages and the colonial system in Africa, see Bill Freund, *The Making of Contemporary Africa* (Westport, Capital City: Greenwood Press, 1985).
15. These events are too well known to need any substantiation and documentation. It was about this period that Marx wrote: " . . . the colonial system ripened, like a hothouse, trade and migration . . . The treasure captured outside Europe by undisguised looting, enslavement and murder, floated back to the mother country and were then turned into capital." (K. Marx, *Capital I*, Ch. XXXI). See Palm Dutt, *Crisis of Empire* (London: Special issue of the Daily Worker, 1950), p. 18.
16. Dutt, Ibid. Between 1880-84 and 1900-04, British export increased 8 percent, German 40 percent, and American 230 percent.
17. Ibid.
18. The most authoritative juristic voice is Grigory Tunkin. See *Contemporary International Law*, Ed. by G. Tunkin and several eminent Soviet jurists contributing. (Moscow: Progress Publishers, 1969).
19. Bobrov points to UN General Assembly resolutions 1514 (xv), 1654 (xvi), 1810 (xvii), 2105 (xx), and 2189 (xxi) as proof of his assertion. See P.L. Bobrov, *Basic Principles of Present Day International Law* in Tunkin (ed) op cit., p. 54.
20. Ibid.
21. Art. 1(1)
22. Art. 1(2)
23. Art. 1(3)
24. Art. 1(4)
25. One treaty they violated was the Kellogg-Briand Pact (Pact of Paris) of August 27, 1928. 4C.Stat.2343, T.S. No. 796, 2 Bevans 732, 99 L.N.T.S. 57.
26. This was specifically entered in the particulars of the offence of the bill of indictment at the Nuremberg trial. Count one indicts "those Nazi leaders who were claimed to bear responsibility for war crimes indicted for conspiracy to wage wars of aggression; count two indicts them for initiating or waging wars of aggression (i.e., crimes against peace); count three indicts them for 'crimes against Humanity.' " Those indicted were: Goring, Hess, Von Ribbentrop, Ley, Keitel, Kaltenbrunner, Rosenberg, Frank, Frick, Streicher, Schacht, Krupp, Donitz, Raeder, Schirach, Sauckel, Jodl, Borman (tried in absentia), von Pappen, Seyss-Inguart, Speer, von Neurath, and Fritzsch. Hundreds of other

war crimes involving lesser Nazi officials were held throughout Europe and ultimately over 3,000 persons were convicted. See B.H. Weston, R.A. Falk, and A.A. D'Amato, *International Law and World Order* (St. Paul, MN:West Publishing Company, 1980).
27. Ibid.
28. See Chapter 4 below on this.
29. To be fair, Roosevelt's view of the colonial empire contrasted sharply with Churchill's. See Elliott Roosevelt, *As He Saw It* (New York: Duel, Sloan and Pearce, 1946) in which the president's son records a sharp exchange between Roosevelt and Churchill at the time of the Atlantic Charter meeting. Churchill is quoted as saying: "Mr. President, I believe you are trying to do away with the British Empire. Every idea you entertain about the structure of the post-war world demonstrates it. But in spite of that, we know that you constitute our only hope. You know that without America the Empire won't stand (p. 41)."
30. All accepted, except Guinea, for which the French punished her by destroying equipment, buildings, and materials throughout Guinea before the French departed.
31. Professor W.I. Jennings, eminent British constitutional lawyer and author of *The Constitutional Laws of the British Empire* (Oxford: Clarendon Press, 1957) explained this change in a letter to *The Times of London* dated June 6, 1949: " 'Empire' was associated with imperialism, which was the deadliest of political sins. The use of Commonwealth made political conditions slightly less difficult."
32. See P. Dutt, op cit., pp. 66-67.
33. Cf. the author's *The Executive in African Governments* (London: Heinemann, 1974).
34. See, for example, resolutions 421D (v), 545 (vi), 637A (vii), 637C (vii), 738 (viii), 837 (ix), 1514 (xv), 1654 (xvi), 1702 (xvi), 1807 (xvii), 2105 (xx), and 2189 (xxi).
35. Bobrov, op. cit.
36. This aspect is discussed in more detail in Chapter 4 below.
37. H. Kelson, *Principles of International Law*, 2nd revised ed., Ed. by Robert Tucker (New York: Holt, Rinehart and Winston, 1966), p. 454.
38. Ibid.
39. Ibid., pp. 454-456.
40. Ibid.
41. Lord McNair, *The Law of Treaties*, 1961, 493-494, quoted in Weston, Falk, and D'Amato, op cit., p. 26.
42. G. Tunkin, *Theory on International Law*, p. 251, trans. by W. Butler, 1974, quoted in Weston, Falk, and D'Amato, op cit., p. 9.
43. For inter-socialist relations, see V.M. Shurshalov, "International Law in Relations Among Socialist Countries," in *Contemporary International Law*, Ed. by G. Tunkin, loc cit., pp. 59-76.
44. W. Friedmann, *The Changing Structure of International Law*, (Columbia University Press, 1964), p. 70.
45. Ibid. Friedmann warns against the rigid diplomatic and political science thinking, on the one side, and "black-letter-law" on the other.

46. Brierly, quoted in R.A. Falk, op cit., p. 66.
47. H.L.A. Hart, *The Concept of Law* (Oxford: Oxford University Press, 1961), pp. 210-211.
48. Ibid.
49. In pursuit of its purposes, the United Nations and its members are required to act in accordance with "the principle of the sovereign equality of all its members [Art 2(1)], and, all of its members are required "to refrain in their international relations from the threat or use of force against the territorial integrity or political independence of any state or in any other manner inconsistent with the purposes of the United Nations" [Art 2(4)].
50. Hart, op cit., 215.
51. Reference is to the author of the idea in English jurisprudence, John Austin, who dominated jurisprudence for a century after he wrote *The Province of Jurisprudence Determined*, 2nd ed. (New York: Burt Franklin, 1970).
52. Hart bases his original arguments on the nature of law on a thesis of law as "the union of primary and secondary rules." See Hart, op cit., Ch 2-5.
53. Ibid., p. 216.
54. Ibid., p. 217.
55. Ibid., p. 218.
56. Ibid., pp. 219-220. See also the contention of Lord McNair in the quoted passage, which is similar to Hart's contention.
57. Bobrov, op cit., p. 50.
58. Cf. K. Nkrumah, *Africa must Unite* (New York: F.A. Praeger, 1963) and also his address to the first meeting of the African heads of states and governments at Addis Ababa, May 1963. See also G.A. Nasser, *Philosophy of the Revolution* (Buffalo, NY: Smith, Keynes and Marshall, 1959).
59. Joseph L. Kunz, "The Changing Law of Nations," *American Journal of International Law* 51 (1957).
60. Bobrov, op cit., p. 50.
61. Cf. M. Akehurst, *A Modern Introduction to International Law* (London: Allen and Unwin, 1977), pp. 31-32.
62. See Richard Barnet, and Ronald Muller, *Global Reach: The Power of the Multinational Corporation* (New York: Simon and Schuster, 1974.)
63. See K. Nkrumah, *Neo-Colonialism: The Last Stage of Imperialism* (New York: International Publishers, 1966).
64. Ibid.
65. R. Falk, op cit., p. 7.
66. The author's experience in the administration of justice attests to such difficulty, particularly at a time when newly codified laws—based on European models—were sought to be applied to a diverse, multi-ethnic Ethiopia with customary laws almost as numerous as the national or ethnic groups.
67. Falk, op cit., p. 67.
68. Outside Europe among nations of Africa and Asia the idea of inter-state relations and peaceful exchange is an old one.

69. UN Charter, Art. 1(4).
70. See, for instance, the resolutions cited Note 34 above, especially resolutions 1514 (xxv) of 1960 and 2625 (xxv) of 1970.
71. These include the Geneva Convention of 1949, the convention on refugees of 1951, and several other instruments on conflict situations.
72. The annual reports of Amnesty International and other human rights organizations which make sad reading are generally too well known to require any documentation here.
73. On the bloc policies of the United Nations see, for example M. Margaret Ball, "Bloc Voting in the General Assembly," in Leland M. Goodrich and David A. Kay, *International Organization: Politics and Process*, Madison: The University of Wisconsin Press, 1973, pp. 77-105.
74. This growth of NGOs may be explained, in part, as an aspect of the failure of the United Nations, exposing a need that must be filled by non-official bodies with a capacity to move faster and speak more freely. It is a response to the challenge posed by the dilemma regarding sovereignty noted above. See, for example, Sadruddin Aga Kahn, "Souverainte des etats et bien-etre de la personne," *Le Monde Diplomatique* (Avril 1986). The Aga Kahn, as a co-president of the Independent Commission on International Humanitarian Questions, explains the reasons for the establishment of the Commission in terms similar to the present discussion.
75. See, for example, George Kim, "Arms and its Consequences for Developing Countries," *Asian-Survey* XXIV.11 (Nov. 1984):1103, which suggests that half of the current balance of payments deficit in the Third World has been caused by arms transfers.
76. Falk makes an important distinction between this kind of pursuit and what he calls "residium of private violence" not satisfied by the institutions of the State. Falk, op cit., p. 68.
77. See, for example, "Democracy and the Question of Nationalism in Ethiopia," *Meskerem, A Marxist-Leninist Theoretical Journal*, Addis Ababa:III.11:88-103.
78. In general, the UN Universal Declaration of Human Rights recognizes the right of national groups as subjects of special protection. For example, Peter Weiss divides human rights into two categories, see his *Human Rights and Basic Needs*, Washington, DC: IPS, 1977.
79. It would be of interest to reproduce now, for the record, Lenin's definition of class. He wrote: "Classes are large groups of people which differ from each other by the place they occupy in a historically defined system of social production, by their relation to the means of production, by their role in the social organization of labor, and consequently, by the dimensions and methods of acquiring the share of social wealth that they obtain. Classes are groups of people one of which may appropriate the labor of another owing to the different places they occupy in the definite system of social economy." (Lenin, *Collected Works*, Vol. 9, pp. 432-433).
80. As a result, negative attitudes toward the United Nations have developed among American conservatives. Official American government attitudes have

not changed significantly, as the continued financial support demonstrates. Recently, however, the American government has shown reluctance in paying its contributions on time. Three acts of Congress have contributed to this. The Kassebaum Amendment, intended to reduce the American share of the UN budget from 25 percent to 20 percent, cuts $42 million. The Sundquist Amendment withholds the American share ($20 million) of the cost of salaries for secretariat staff (mostly Soviet nationals) who allegedly remit part of their pay to the government. And then there is the Gramm-Rudmann-Hollings Amendment which orders an across-the-board cut. See the *Washington Post*, May 4, 1986, editorial entitled "U.N. Squeeze."

81. As the *Washington Post* editorially admonishes the American government: "The Reagan Administration wants to be known as committed to internationalism, but it still rebels against the familiar frustrations of dealing in the world organization. It wants less expense and more influence. It has to figure out which it wants more." Ibid.
82. Mohamed Bedjanoui is now a judge in the International Court of Justice.
83. This is a free rendering of the French: "une espece de simple *modus vivendi* entre l'Est et l'Ouest sans la moindre volonte de realizer un modele universel pour instaurer et developper des rapports de collaboration entre tous les Etats par-dela les differences de systemes politiques et sociaux." Bedjaoui, op cit., p. 364.
84. The OAU is divided on the Western Sahara issue, with a majority supporting POLISARIO. And the Eritrean issue has not yet found itself on the OAU agenda.
85. Examples are Malta and the Philippines. See Bedjaoui, op cit., pp. 366-367.
86. See Chapter 6 below.
87. See preamble of the Charter.

Chapter 2
Eritrea and the United Nations

A COLONY SINGLED OUT FOR DENIAL OF INDEPENDENCE

Introduction: The United Nations and Self-Determination

The United Nations is, or should be, a conscience of the international community, if not much else. And there is no subject on which it has been more sorely tested in that regard than the question of self-determination of Eritrea.

One of the purposes of the United Nations as defined in Article 1 of the charter is to "develop friendly relations among nations based on respect for the principle of equal rights and self-determination of peoples." Article 55 of the charter also calls for the creation of conditions of stability and well-being necessary for peaceful and friendly relations among nations based on the principle of equal rights and self-determination. The right to self-determination has been further elaborated in several United Nations decisions and has formed the basis for some actions by the United Nations and its organs. The whole process of decolonization in the post-World War II period has been articulated in terms of the principle of self-determination.

In 1950, the General Assembly of the United Nations reaffirmed the fundamental rights of peoples and nations to self-determination and called upon the Economic and Social Council to request the Commission of Human rights "to study ways and means which would assure the right of peoples and nations to self-determination." Ironically, that was the same year that the General Assembly passed a resolution which in effect denied the Eritrean people the benefit of a principle applied universally to all other former colonial peoples.

Again, the General Assembly, at its 1951-1952 session, decided to include in the International Covenants on Human Rights: "an article on the right of all peoples and nations to self-determination in re-affirmation of the principle enunciated in the Charter of the United Nations." The General Assembly insisted that the article should include the terms: "*All peoples shall have the right to self-determination.*" The following year (1952) at its seventh session, the General Assembly adopted a resolution in which it recognized that the right of peoples and nations to self-determination is a prerequisite to the full enjoyment of all fundamental human rights and that every United Nations member shall respect that right. That same year the UN resolution which forcibly "federated" Eritrea with Ethiopia [Resolution 390 A(V)] came into effect, ushering in another era of struggle for the Eritrean people. Why were the Eritrean people thus victimized and denied the same right which the United Nations repeatedly and emphatically affirmed as a universal principle? The answer is linked to the strategic and geopolitical interests of the United States of America and its Western allies at the time. In order to gain a proper understanding of this question we have to trace the history of the period relevant to Eritrea and summarize the salient issues.

From the Treaty of Paris to the UN Debates
The Treaty of Paris and Four Power Disagreement

Italian colonial rule in Eritrea came to an end militarily in the spring of 1941, after the defeat of the Italian colonial army by British and Allied forces. Diplomatically, Italian rule ended with the signing of the Treaty of Peace with Italy signed in Paris in July 1946, in which Italy renounced her claims to her former colonial possessions including Eritrea. The Paris Treaty was signed 57 years after Eritrea became an Italian colony, in 1889 following the signing of the Italo-Ethiopian Treaty (the Treaty of Ucciale) under which the Ethiopian emperor, Menelik, recognized the present border between Ethiopia and Eritrea. The British, who favored Italian (as against French) advances in the region, now became the principal agents in the demise of Italian colonial rule, and temporarily stepped into Italian shoes.

Britain occupied Eritrea from 1941 to 1952. During that period several attempts were made to partition Eritrea with the aim of joining the western and northern parts to the then British-held Sudan, and joining the southern and eastern coastal region, including the ports of Massaw and Assab to Emperor Haile Selassie's Ethiopia. Emperor Haile Selassie's expansionist ambitions involved not only a desire to control the outlet to the Red Sea, but quite simply territorial aggrandizement. He was aware of Eritrea's mineral wealth and comparatively more advanced industrial and skilled manpower resources which he wanted to appropriate.

Emperor Haile Selassie's expansionist ambitions are further illustrated by his claiming not only Eritrea but also former Italian Somaliland. This claim was first put forward by the emperor when he visited President Franklin D. Roosevelt at Great Bitter Lake in early 1945 seeking Roosevelt's help in putting pressure on the British. The claim was repeated a few times thereafter, including at the Paris Conference in July 1946 and in New York during the second part of the First UN Session (October 23 through December 15, 1946).

The question of the future of the former Italian colonies was first formally discussed during the Paris Peace Conference in July 1946, even though it had been the subject of conversation and negotiation among some of the Four Powers (the Big Four)—the USA, the USSR, Great-Britain, and France. Article 23 of the Treaty of Paris stipulated that the final disposal of the former Italian colonies be determined by agreement among the Four Powers. In the event of failure of agreement among the Four Powers within one year, the matter would be submitted to the General Assembly of the United Nations for disposition. The Four Powers did fail to agree on this matter by the deadline date (September 15, 1947). In November 1947, a Four-Power commission of investigation was established to visit the three former Italian territories (Libya, Eritrea, and Italian Somaliland) and to report on the political situation. The commission submitted this report in May 1948, but there was no basis on which the Four Powers could agree.

One basis on which they should have found a common ground would have been to give the Eritrean people the right to determine their future in a referendum. Ethiopia was opposed to this because it was known that the majority of the Eritrean people wanted independence. Britain was also opposed. British opposition was based on two grounds: first, its immediate aim to partition Eritrea and annex a large part to the Sudan; the second, and perhaps more important, reason concerned the long-term implications to the British colonial empire if there were an exercise of self-determination by popular referendum. That went against the grain of "controlled change," which Britain consistently followed subsequently.

The whole question was submitted to the Third session of the General Assembly in April 1949.

The Third Session and the Bevin-Sforza Plan

The Bevin-Sforza plan is an aspect of the continued disagreement among the four powers regarding the final disposal of the former Italian colonies. It also reflects changing patterns of relationship between former enemies —Britain and Italy. The plan worked out between the British Foreign Secretary, Ernest Bevin, and the Italian Minister of Foreign Affairs, Count Sforza, proposed the following. Libya was to be divided into three parts: Cyrenaica, to be under British rule; Fezan, to be under French rule; and Tripolitania, to be under Italian rule. Somaliland would also be administered by Italy, while Eritrea was to be partitioned along the lines indicated above. The United States agreed to the plan with one qualification: Cyrenaica would be under British rule, while decision on the Fezan and Tripolitania would be postponed.

Partition of Eritrea suited the British and it suited Emperor Haile Selassie as the second best option to satisfy his imperial ambition. Documents of the State Department that have since come to light reveal that US policy backed the two positions (British and imperial Ethiopian) regarding Eritrea, which the Bevin-Sforza plan included in a larger package. One such document states:

> The United States and the United Kingdom have (similarly) agreed to support the cession to Ethiopia of all of Eritrea except the Western province. The United States has given assurances to Ethiopia in this regard. Such a cession would be accompanied by guarantees by Ethiopia of minority rights and of the return of former Italian settlers.[1]

As for Cyrenaica, the same document states that the United States is committed to British rule under a trusteeship for Cyrenaica because this would " ... provide the best assurance that the United Kingdom would retain control of its bases and facilities in Cyrenaica."

The Third Session of the UN General Assembly debated the question of the disposal of the three former Italian colonies. The first stage of the debate was in the First Committee (the political committee) which took place between April 6 and May 13, 1949. As regards Eritrea, the prevailing view of the committee was in favor of partition, reflecting the pressure of the US-UK alliance. The second stage of the debate took place in the plenary session of the General Assembly on May 17 and 18, 1949. The plenary session reviewed the whole question on the basis of the report of the First Committee. The Bevin-Sforza plan was subjected to merciless attacks. Delegates of Poland, Iraq, Byelorussia SSR, and the Ukraine SSR charged that private negotiations between the United Kingdom and Italy took place in disregard of international opinion and that the report of the subcommittee (A/C1/466) which formed the basis of the report of the first committee was merely a paraphrase of the Bevin-Sforza agreement.[2]

At the same time the Eritreans were united in their emphatic rejection of the idea of partition. The idea fell through because of the combination of this rejection and the disagreement within the UN body itself. The question was postponed to the fourth session.

The Fourth UN Session and the Commision of Enquiry
United States Strategic Interests and Ethiopian Demands: A Unity of Interests

At the fourth session of the UN General Assembly the future of Libya and former Italian Somaliland was decided—Libya to be granted independence by January 1952, and Somalia to be under a ten-year Italian trusteeship after which it would accede to independence. The General Assembly failed to reach agreement on Eritrea. It therefore decided to send a second commission of enquiry composed of five members, representing Burma, Guatemala, Norway, Pakistan, and South Africa.[3] The commission was charged with the duty of ascertaining "the wishes of the Eritrean people and the means of promoting their future welfare."[4]

The off-stage intrigues of interested parties was dominated by US (and Western) strategic interests in the Red Sea area. In point of fact those interests operated to frustrate the "wishes of the Eritrean people and the means of promoting their future welfare" which the General Assembly had charged the Commission to find out. At the very moment when the UN decided to send the commission of enquiry, US policymakers were busy working out ways and means of gaining and maintaining strategic control of the area.

A letter written by the US secretary of defense, James Forrestal, to Secretary of State Dean Acheson illustrates this. Forrestal wrote:

> From the standpont of strategic and logistical considerations it would be [of] value to the United States to have refineries, capable of supplying a substantial portion of our aviation needs, located close to a crude supply and also close to areas where naval task forces would be operating and where airfields would be located, yet far enough removed to be reasonably safe from effective enemy bombing.
>
> With respect to the Middle East, refineries located in Italian Somaliland and Eritrea would meet the foregoing conditions . . . therefore,

as a long-range provision of potential military value, it is believed that concession on rights should be sought for United States interests to construct and operate refineries in Italian Somaliland and Eritrea. These rights should include necessary transportation and port concessions, together with air and naval base rights and communication facilities.[5]

The letter goes on to give a glimpse of things to come—of the agreement between the United States and Emperor Haile Selassie. Forrestal argues:

> It would appear that demands by our probable enemies for concessions of like nature would be invited if efforts were made by the United States to include the matter of concessions to us in prospective United Nations agreements for the disposition of former Italian colonies. This would obviously be undesirable from the military viewpoint. It would, however, be satisfactory from the military viewpoint if the matter could be handled by separate agreement with friendly nations desiring control of Italian Somaliland and Eritrea.

It is obvious who the "friendly nations" were that Secretary Forrestal had in mind. Less than four months later Aklilu Habtewold, the then vice-minister of foreign affairs of Ethiopia, visited Secretary of State Dean Acheson at the State Department, accompanied by his American legal advisor, John Spencer, one of the architects of Ethiopian foreign policy for many years. A recently released document shows the emerging pattern of a mutuality of interests between the American and Ethiopian governments. One pertinent passage of the document reads:

> The Secretary (Acheson) expressed the pleasure of the American Government at the military facilities which the Emperor indicated he would grant to the U.S. in Eritrea after that area has been ceded to Ethiopia. Mr. Aklilu responded that the emperor was pleased to be of help in this matter. Still speaking in the name of the emperor, Mr. Aklilu expressed satisfaction at the assignment of an American military attache to the Mission in Addis Ababa and with the elevation of that mission to the rank of Embassy.[6]

American policy was thus wedded to the idea of meeting Ethiopian demands, as a *quid pro quo* for strategic interests in Eritrea. State Department internal memoranda issued as guidelines for the US delegation at the General Assembly were clear-cut on this issue.[7] In every instance, strategic and geopolitical factors, not the welfare or aspirations of the Eritrean people, were the primary considerations. Indeed, at times the aspirations of the former colonizers were invoked as relevant. For example, the same internal memo, dealing with the disposal of former Italian Somaliland, states that the US recommendation of Italian trusteeship for Italian Somaliland "is based chiefly on the desirability of giving some recognition to the needs and aspirations of the Italian people with respect to their former colonies.[8]

It was against this background of behind-the-scenes "deals" that the UN Commission of Enquiry was sent on a mission which was predetermined to a strategic objective.

The Report of the UN Commission of Enquiry and Resolution 390 A(V): A Denial of Self-Determination

The UN Commission presented its report on June 28, 1949. The report was as follows. The majority—the representatives of Burma, Norway, and South Africa—recommended a close association of Eritrea under Ethiopian sovereignty, while Norway recommended unconditional union with Ethiopia. The minority report—Guatemala and Pakistan—recommended a United Nations trusteeship over Eritrea for ten years, after which Eritrea would become independent. Both majority and minority reports opposed partition, thus fairly and accurately reflecting Eritrean sentiments.

This last point involves perhaps the only matter on which the Eritrean peoples' views were heard and fairly represented, despite the US/UK machinations to make partition a reality. The majority report succumbed to such machinations and distorted information when it concluded, for example, that Eritrea was not capable of establishing a viable economy, a factor which it considered of decisive importance in its decision. Such a conclusion, which flies in the face of the facts, was influenced by the opinions of the "Administering Power" (occupying power), which had control of all economic and other data on Eritrea. The opinion of the British on this matter was revealed by the remarks of the British delegate to the United Nations General Assembly in the debate at the Ad Hoc Political Committee.

Britain as the occupying power had significant leverage to influence the outcome of events in the Eritrean question, manipulating facts and issues in a given direction. To take the crucial example of demographics, the UN Commission of Enquiry was led to believe that the Eritrean population was divided between Christians and Moslems and that the majority (Christians) favored union with Ethiopia. The belief was fostered by the occupying power with a predetermined end in view. Yet, the facts were, that despite some religious tensions here and there many of which were exploited by the British, most Eritreans (Christians and Moslems) were united in their goal of freedom and independence. Again, some documents have come to light attesting to the reality of the undue influence and manipulative role of the British on the UN Commission of Enquiry. For example, a telegram sent from the US Embassy in Addis Ababa to Washington, marked "confidential," contains the following passage:

> Keren branch of the Unionist Party has defected en bloc. British administrator estimates privately for British Embassy Addis that independence bloc commands 75 per cent of Eritrea as of August 10.[9]

It should be noted here that the Eritrean bloc for independence, composed of 8 political parties and associations, had asked the UN General Assembly, during its Third Session, for immediate independence.

Another interesting part of the same telegram reveals the nature of the Unionist party (the pro-Ethiopia party). It reads:

> According to British Embassy, defections from Unionist Party in Eritrea are causing concerns in Ethiopian Government. Under guise of vacations and health visits party of Ethiopian ministers ... recently traveled (to) Asmara and were, according (to) Brigadier Drew, British Administrator, engaged active propaganda. Unionists are understood by Drew to have threatened wholesale defection to independence bloc unless Ethiopia accord immediate and substantial support and guidance. Unionists asked Deressa (Ethiopian minister) "How many cabinet seats will Eritrea get and how many seats in Chamber of Deputies will be accorded us."[10]

The leadership of the Unionst party is seen here for what it was: a self-seeking group of power-brokers with no mass support and representing narrow, selfish interests. Trevaskis has written that the Unionist party leadership were "servants of the Ethiopian Government"[11] and not free agents; small wonder that Ethiopia (and Britain) consistently opposed any suggestion of self-determination by way of referendum. As for Ethiopia, their UN delegation had shown strong opposition even to the idea of a commission of enquiry to be sent by the United Nations.

The telegram also reports that the first convention of the Eritrean independence bloc, held in Asmara on August 10, 1949 resolved to send a message to "all freedom loving countries" to support the Eritrean demand for independence. The message stated that "local economic and technical resources should serve only Eritrean well-being and not foreigners, whatever their race." The US Embassy official who sent the telegram adds:

> Whether this was intended (to) mean denial of radio, port and air facilities to U.S. and allies is problematical but may mean Italian influence of independence bloc is overrated, as Embassy presumes any pro-Italian group would be in touch Rome where such a statement would be unlikely at this time.[12]

Aside from every other consideration, the clear position of the Eritrean independence bloc on the future of Eritrean economic and other resources, expressed in the telegram, would have been enough to alienate it from any support of the United States or the occupying power. In 1949 that kind of economic (over and above political) nationalism was anathema to the colonial and the emerging imperialist interests. British manipulation of events, issues, and facts in Eritrea must be seen in light of these interests.

Britain, as the administering Power, used its leverage to influence the outcome of events in the Eritrean question. As already noted, the British threw their lot in support of the Ethiopian claim, at the behest of the United States of America. The United States, which emerged as the dominant economic and military power after World War II, was not getting involved in the Korean War. When the Korean War broke out on June 25, 1950, Britain was a weakened imperial power, with its domestic economy in shambles and a diminishing international role.

The debate on the divided report of the UN Commission of Enquiry on Eritrea took place in a political atmosphere dominated by the Korean War. The Eritrean question was seen in a new light for an expanding American imperialist role, which was fast replacing the British role in many areas of the world. Aklilu Habtewold, the Ethiopian minister of foreign affairs at the time, has since boastfully claimed that Haile Selassie's diplomacy exploited the cold war by openly staking the future and fortune of Ethiopia on the side of the Western powers led by the United States, in return for a "deal" on Eritrea.[13]

Ethiopia's commitment on the side of the West was fulfilled in more ways than one. Haile Selassie sent a battalion of his well-trained Imperial Bodyguard to fight on the US side in the Korean War. Another dramatic illustration of the changing roles in the imperial game, showing the United States to be the ascendant imperialist power, was the grant of the Kagnew communications base near Asmara. The United States and Emperor Haile Selassie signed a secret agreement lasting for twenty-five years, under which the United States "leased" the Kagnew base, and Haile Selassie obtained military and other assistance.[14] The agreement represents the legal high-water-mark in the process of US neocolonization of Ethiopia, turning Eritrea into a colony of a neocolony. The agreement is replete with examples of how the emperor abjectly reduced Ethiopia to a neocolony.[15]

As we have seen, Emperor Haile Selassie placed himself at the disposal of the United States which, in return, maneuvered the United Nations to push for a "federal" solution for Eritrea. This is the background against which United Nations Resolution 390 A(v) was passed on December 2, 1950, proposing that Eritrea be constituted as an autonomous unit to be federated with Ethiopia under the sovereignty of the Ethiopian Crown. This was clearly in violation of the United Nations Charter and contrary to the wishes of the Eritrean people for self-determination.

SALIENT FEATURE OF RESOLUTION 390 A(V)

Federation Under Imperial Sovereignty
An Autonomous Unit Under Imperial Crown

The United Nations Resolution provided for an autonomous Eritrean government with legislative, executive, and judicial powers over domestic affairs, with matters of defense, foreign affairs, currency and finance, foreign and "interstate" trade and communications falling under "federal" (or Ethiopian) jurisdiction. In the interim period between December 1950 and September 1952, a UN commission would be appointed to prepare a draft constitution for Eritrea and submit it to an Eritrean constituent assembly to be convened by the British "administering authority."

It should be noted here that the Soviet Union, along with nine other members of the United Nations, opposed the "federal" solution, proposing instead complete independence for Eritrea in accordance with the provisions of the UN Charter.

The preamble of the Resolution which set out the supposed rationale is a travesty of justice. It reads, in part:

> Taking into consideration (a) the wishes and welfare of the inhabitants of Eritrea, including the views of the various racial, religious and political groups of the provinces of the territory and the capacity the people for self-government; (b) the interests of peace and security in East Africa; (c) the rights and claims of Ethiopia based on geographical, historical, ethnic or economic reasons, including in particular Ethiopia's legitimate need for adequate access to the sea... Desiring that this association [of Eritrea with Ethiopia] assures to the

inhabitants of Eritrea *the fullest respect and safeguards for their institutions, traditions, religions and languages, as well as the widest possible measure of self-government* . . . (emphasis added)

The inconsistency inherent in this legal language is evident. How can "the interests of peace" be secured when a basic condition has been denied, that is, the exercise of the right of self-determination of the people, which right the United Nations arrogated to itself? How could a world body that took into consideration "the wishes and welfare of the inhabitants of Eritrea" arrive at a decision which denied those wishes? Was it necessary to fabricate (or to endorse the Ethiopian fabrication of) "historical reasons," in order to advance the interests of Ethiopia? Was Ethiopia's "legitimate" need for adequate access to the sea in itself sufficient to cause the denial of the right of the Eritrean people to self-determination? Ethiopia is not, after all, the only nation which has a need to access to the sea.

The real reason of course lies elsewhere, as already noted. John Foster Dulles, put it bluntly. Speaking before the United Nations Security Council as the head of the US delegation to the United Nations in 1950, he said:

> From the point of view of justice, the opinions of the Eritrean people must receive consideration. Nevertheless the strategic interest of the United States in the Red Sea basin and considerations of security and world peace make it necessary that the country has to be linked with our ally, Ethiopia.[16]

The phrasing of Dulles's statement is significant. The word "nevertheless," coming as it does after the sentence which recognizes the right of the Eritrean people, provides additional evidence that the United States knew the wishes of the Eritrean people to be decisively for independence.

The Eritrean people were thus launched upon a new form of "colonial" rule under the guise of federation. The United Nations Commissioner Anze Matienzo, who was responsible for drafting the Eritrean constitution, spent many weeks negotiating with the emperor and members of his government on some of the provisions of the draft constitution. The chief obstacle was the fact that the emperor's government was a feudal one with no democratic pretensions, whereas the Eritrean constitution was of bourgeois, democratic inspiration.

Ivor Jennings, the eminent British constitutional lawyer, was one of the four-member panel of jurists appointed by UN Commissioner Anze Matienzo to draft a constitution for Eritrea. Jennings has written about the dilemma facing the panel of jurists who sat at the Palais des Nations in

Geneva to draft a Constitution for Eritrea pursuant to the UN resolution.[17] The dilemma was how to work out a constitution, as he put it, "for a democratic state federally united with Ethiopia."[18]

Jennings cites Jeremy Bentham as authority for the view that there were fundamental principles which enabled any jurist to work out a constitutional scheme for any country, provided that he was given information about its social, political, and economic conditions. In this case (Eritrea) such information was supplied under the auspices of the UN Commissioner.

Absence of Crucial Elements of the Federal Principle

The constitutional anomaly was further aggravated by the absence of an essential principle of the federal idea. That is, there must be equality among the component parts of the federation, with a "neutral" arbiter to settle any conflicts that might arise between or among them. In this case Eritrea was not only unequal to Ethiopia, but there was no provision made to mediate conflicts.

Anze Matienzo's formula for resolving the constitutional anomaly was to suggest that Ethiopia revise its feudal constitution (of 1931), updating it with some democratic trappings. This was the origin of the Revised Constitution of 1955. Matienzo's democratic conscience, such as it was, must have constantly pricked him in view of his knowledge that, politically, Eritrea was a much more developed country than Ethiopia and that a democratic society was forcibly wedded to a feudal autocracy in a lopsided federal scheme of unequal partnership with no "neutral" arbiter. Perhaps this explains the interesting paragraph in his final report:

> With regard to the application of the General Assembly's resolution after the entry into force of the Federal Act and the Constitution of Eritrea, the panel (of jurists) expressed the following view: "It is true that once the Federal Act and the Eritrean Constitution have come into force the mission entrusted to the General Assembly under the Peace Treaty with Italy will have been fulfilled and that the future of Eritrea must be regarded as settled, but it does not follow that the United Nations would no longer have any right to deal with the question. The United Nations Resolution of Eritrea would remain an international instrument and, if violated, the General Assembly could be seized of the matter."[19]

As it happened, the resolution was violated almost immediately after the federation was put into effect. Matienzo's cautionary remarks might be seen as prophetic, but for the fact that they were made by a man who knew the intentions and predelictions of the Ethiopian government. The emperor's spies and saboteurs were conducting smear campaigns and acts of terror against leading Eritrean personalities deep in Eritrean territory with British knowledge. Anze Matienzo had occasion to hear petitions from aggrieved Eritreans and thus gain a clear insight into the unsatisfied ambitions of the emperor. The "federal" scheme was only a betrothal scheme which merely whetted the imperial appetite to violate its terms and swallow up Eritrea.

Recognition of Eritrea Under International Law
Legal Status of Eritrea—Realities and Ambiguities

The seeds of conflict were sown by the United Nations General Assembly with Resolution 390 A(v). The panel of jurists agonized over the constitutional incompatibility of a democratic state wedded to a more powerful, feudal empire; but they had to work out a constitutional scheme within the framework of the resolution. The opinion they gave, to which Matienzo referred in his above-cited report, reflects their uneasiness over the whole arrangement.

To begin with, there was the problem of the legal status of the Eritrean nation. The UN resolution glossed over that fundamental question, even though implied recognition is given to the Eritreans as a colonial people. Ethiopian claims to the contrary notwithstanding, Eritrea has not formed part of Ethiopia. Ethiopia itself is the creation of imperial conquest and expansion of the late nineteenth century. The expansion started from the central highland kingdom of Shoa under King Menelik. Eritrea, in its present borders, came into being as a parallel development to Menelik's southward imperial expansion, at the same time Italy was forging its new colony. The two empires (Italian and Ethiopian) recognized each other, and modern Eritrea was born as a colony under the Treaty of Ucciale (1889).

The manner of disposal of Eritrea by the United Nations, albeit an unfortunate one, itself implicitly recognized the Eritrean people as a colonial people, with all the characteristics that the term implies. Like other colonized peoples elsewhere the Eritrean people were subjected to the same colonial politico-economic order out of which emerged a common sense of nationhood, a new industrial urban working class and other social forces.

Eritrean territorial unity was also recognized after the failure of partition attempts. The resolution refers to Eritrea as an autonomous unit federated to Ethiopia; it speaks of the Eritrean people, of the Eritrean constitution, of

Eritrean assembly, of Eritrean administration, etc.[20] This represents a clear recognition of Eritrea and the Eritrean people under international law, despite the denial of independence.

Rights and Remedies—Inadequate Provision

Despite their recognition under international law, the Eritrean people were bereft of remedies in case of violations of rights granted them under the UN resolution. In other words, they became subject of rights but not of remedies; or as Alain Fenet put it, they were "titulaire de droits mais non suject du droit."[21]

We must distinguish between two sets of rights. First there is the right of the Eritrean people individually considered. These rights were provided for under the Eritrean constitution and the Federal Act. We find these provisions on the fundamental democratic and human rights listed in the UN Charter and the Universal Declaration of Human Rights of 1948. Among the anomalies referred to above, none was more striking than the fact that an Eritrean was subject to these rights, whereas an Ethiopian had no similar rights. Even the Revised Constitution of Ethiopia, promulgated in 1955, was a far cry from that of Eritrea in this respect.

Then there was the other kind of right concerning the Eritrean people as a whole vis-a-vis other peoples or nations—the international legal status of the Eritrean people. This was absent as a result of the denial of self-determination, of independence. In short, its absence is a result of the absence of sovereignty. The legal consequence, within the framework of UN Resolution 390 A(v), of the Federal Act and of the Eritrean Constitution was that whereas Eritreans as individuals or groups had rights and commensurate remedies, Eritreans as a people did not. Any remedy implies a potential breach of right. The "federal" arrangement did not provide for a clear remedy in the event of violation of its terms. Yet it does not make legal sense to work out such an elaborate scheme and not provide remedies to redress violation of the terms and conditions of the scheme. This question will be taken up in more detail below, when discussing the violation of the Resolution and laws made thereunder.

The Federal Act and the Eritrean Constitution
Democratic Institutions Harnessed to Feudal Power

The imperial Ethiopian government felt uncomfortable with the UN arrangement, from the beginning. The implications of a democratic unit grafted onto a feudal system was like an antibody imposed on a body politic that was not able and willing to receive it. During the final debates of the UN General Assembly before the vote of December 2, 1950, Aklilu Habtewold, the Ethiopian foreign minister, after opposing the federal solution had finally accepted it but gave hints of future events when he declared that the federal solution was accepted by Ethiopia only "in the spirit of compromise." From the first moment after the British left, the emperor's government was clearly bent on violating the federal arrangement and annexing Eritrea. The emperor's representative set out systematically to undermine the Eritrean constitution's democratic principles and put the Eritrean government under his control.

Eritrean Jurisdiction: The preamble of Resolution 390 a(v) shows the UN General Assembly desirous that the association of Eritrea with Ethiopia should "assure the inhabitants of Eritrea the fullest respect and safeguards for their institutions, traditions, religions, and languages, as well as the widest possible measure of self-government, while at the same time respecting the constitution, institutions, traditions and the international status and identity of the Empire of Ethiopia." The Eritrean government, which was given legislative, executive, and judicial powers in the field of Eritrean affairs, issued out of an election based on universal adult suffrage. Its jurisdiction included the various branches of law, the organization of the public services, internal police, health, education, public assistance and social security, protection of labor, exploitation of natural resources and regulation of industry, internal commerce, trades and professions, agriculture, internal communications, the public utility services peculiar to Eritrea, the Eritrean budget and the establishment and collection of taxes designed to meet the expenses of Eritrean public function and services.[22]

Democratic and Human Rights: The striking feature of the Eritrean government was that it was based on what Article 16 of the Eritrean constitution called "principles of democratic government." All persons were guaranteed the enjoyment of human rights and fundamental freedoms[23] guaranteed politically and institutionally by means of "periodic free and fair elections, directly and indirectly," and by the requirement that "the organs of government shall act in the interests of the people." It was to be a government of law and not of men, unlike the Ethiopian government in which the emperor was above the law, his powers unlimited and indisputable. The Eritrean constitution provided for the rule of law, as limiting public powers as follows:

> The organs of government and public officials shall have no further powers than those conferred on them by the Constitution and by the laws and regulations which give effect to them.[25]

This principle was buttressed by a detailed provision of a Bill of Rights and fundamental freedoms.[26] The foundation of these rights and freedoms was the democratic principle enshrined in Article 16, and the constitution-makers agreed that Article 16 was not to be amended under any circumstances.[27]

Inherent Contradictions Leading to Violations

The marriage of democratic ideas and institutions to an imperial and feudal power was a fatal combination. It was fatal given the weakness of Eritrea and the absence of clear remedies in this "federal" scheme. The imperial connection was expressed primarily through federal jurisdiction over defense, foreign affairs, currency and finance, foreign and interstate commerce, and external and interstate communications, including ports. The emperor had a representative in Eritrea, with formal constitutional functions of a figurehead of State. But the nation of the government he represented, its power and ambitious designs, foreshadowed a more significant role for the emperor's representative than was warranted by the Federal Act and the Eritrean constitution.

The role of the emperor's representative was meant to be merely formal, according to the federal arrangement—to promulgate legislation enacted by the Eritrean Assembly and to read imperial speeches or messages. The only substantive legal power he possessed lay in his right to return to the Eritrean Assembly legislation which he considered to encroach on federal (Ethiopian) jurisdiction. But the first representative, Andargachew Messai, the emperor's son-in-law, saw his role as being much more than that, and the emperor fully backed him in his campaigns to break Eritrean national will and violate the terms of the United Nations resolution.

Two facts contributed to this attitude and the violations: first, the inordinate ambition of emperor Haile Selassie to incorporate Eritrea as an integral part of his feudal empire; second, the feudal structure in Ethiopia which was anti-democratic. The expansionist amibition was a function of the empire. And the imperial appetite (for expansion) was compounded by the fear and uncertainty of a feudal regime harnessed to a modern bourgeois democratic government. One had to prevail over the other. As it turned out, the imperial ambition was backed by military power and external diplomatic recognition and encouragement.

SYSTEMATIC VIOLATIONS OF RESOLUTION 390 A(V) AND LAWS THEREUNDER

Instances of Violations

Violation of Democratic and Human Rights

The emperor did not waste any time in making his intentions clear. The primary target for attack in the imperial strategy was the democratic principle underlying the Eritrean government.

The Eritrean government, headed by Tedla Bairou, found itself at loggerheads with the emperor's representative. The latter made the imperial intention explicit in a speech he delivered to the Eritrean Assembly on March 22, 1955, in which he said:

> There is no internal or external affairs, as far as the office of his imperial majesty's representative is concerned, and there will be none in the future. The affairs of Eritrea concern Ethiopia as a whole and the emperor.[28]

It was clear that imperial will was being imposed on the democratically formed Eritrean government, contrary to the letter and spirit of the UN Resolution, the Federal Act and the Eritrean constitution. This was accompanied by systematic subversion of the Eritrean government at critical levels. The emperor used his powers as head of state of the "federation" and his powers of appointment to undermine the integrity of the Eritrean government. Tedla Bairou was pressured to resign his post as chief executive and appointed ambassador to Sweden, four months after the above-quoted statement of the emperor's representative was made. Other critics and opponents of the imperial designs were either jailed or exiled.

The democratic principle, the foundation of the Eritrean government—a principle which could not be amended constitutionally—was thus subverted extra-constitutionally. The rule of law was gradually replaced by the rule of men, with the extension of feudal and imperial power to Eritrea. But not without resistance. The mass of Eritrean workers, students, and teachers protested. Their protest was met with further violation of fundamental human rights—shootings, arbitrary arrests, and even the banning of labor union activities and the closing of industries. The latter was designed first to weaken Eritrea economically and retroactively prove their point about Eritrea's nonviability as an economy, and secondly to strike at the Eritrean labor movement which was an organized and effective national political force. These measures drove thousands of

Eritreans out of their homeland in search of employment elsewhere. But they failed in breaking the back of organized labor.

Meanwhile Tedla was replaced by Asfaha Wolde-Mikael, an imperial crony. Tedla's resignation was followed by that of the president of the Eritrean Assembly, whose work was made impossible by the emperor's representative. He was replaced by a weak president who was dominated by the vice-president, Dimetros Gabre-Mariam, an Orthodox cleric fanatically pro-Ethiopia. This and the continued violation of the terms of the UN resolution and the Eritrean constitution led to more mass protests. The internal process was spurred on by external broadcasts made by some of the exiled Eritrean leaders like Wolde-Ab Wolde-Mariam, the leader of the pro-independence party and president of Eritrean labor unions.

Suppression of Local Institutions, Culture, and Languages

At this point it is worth recalling the United Nations resolution on this topic. The preamble shows the UN General Assembly anxious to assure Eritreans "the fullest respect and safeguards for their institutions, traditions, religions and languages, as well as the widest possible measure of government." It was on these and other terms and conditions that the UN resolved that Eritrea should constitute an autonomous unit federated with Ethiopia. Yet barely five years after the "federation" came into force, Amharic replaced Tigrigna and Arabic as a language of official communication and of instruction. This not only violated the UN resolution and the Eritrean constitution, but imposed a painful obstacle to the learning abilities of Eritrean children. The effects of such disabilities were reflected some years later in secondary and university entrance examinations, which barred the way of thousands of Eritreans to higher education. As students were affected, everybody else was affected. The students brought back home with them the militancy of aggrieved youth, and this in turn fed an already aggrieved national sentiment.

Eritrean Protests and Denial of Remedies
Petitions, Demonstrations, and Strike Actions

Protests began taking massive and more organized forms. Throughout 1956 students intermittently boycotted classes, and upon the suppression of Tigrigna and Arabic and the imposition of Amharic in 1957, students took to the streets. Fighting with the police and other forms of violence became common occurrences.

At the same time Eritrean elders followed the path of the law, presenting petitions to the emperor and his representative. The elders comprised the most respected and advanced members of the Eritrean leadership organized in an effort to agitate in an extra-parliamentary forum, but within the bounds of law. In these efforts they were legally covered by provisions for freedom of speech, association, and assembly guaranteed in the Eritrean constitution and the Federal Act. The boldest among them, and the most politically conscious, explained to the emperor's representative that extra-legal action would be inevitable if the law were violated with impunity. The emperor's representative listened and black-listed.

He was also busy developing joint ventures with foreign and local businessmen. He used business as a weapon to attract some of the more enterprising elements in the emergent bourgeoisie to blunt the Eritrean national consciousness. Thus emerged a small but powerful bourgeoisie which formed the nucleus of a larger satellite of collaborators who were brought by small imperial handouts: government positions, land grants, and other emoluments. The Eritrean chief executive (Asfaha), the vice-president of the Assembly (Dimetros) and the Eritrean chief of police formed the top government circle which presided over this development, with the emperor's representative providing the imperial umbrella. Government power and police terror were employed to secure the advancement of the imperial objective—annexation.

In 1958 the workers of Eritrea organized a general strike and led the mass of urban small businessmen, students, and teachers in one of the bloodiest demonstrations in recent African history. The strike and demonstration followed five years of systematic police terror under a preventive detention law, and the failure of peaceful petitions. Wolde-Ab's broadcasts from Cairo had fired the national anger and broadened the horizon of resistance. Although Emperor Haile Selassie made a "deal" with President Nasser to stop the broadcasts, the message had been delivered loud and clear, and in a language which every Eritrean understood and could easily remember.

Conspiracy of Silence

There was hardly any reporting of the events in Eritrea. Even the labor strike and demonstration which left scores of people dead and hundreds injured was passed over without comment in the world outside. The exiled Eritreans organized a short-lived protest movement which saw some people travelling to petition the United Nations. None could get close to the UN headquarters where the Ethiopian mission to the UN was backed to the hilt by US policy.

Eritreans were instructed by this experience of rejection or betrayal by the international community in the face of blatant violations of international and domestic law perpetrated by the Ethiopian government. One of the lessons which Eritreans have learned is the importance of internal resources. Their emphatic demands for self-determination had been rejected in 1950. They were forced into a compromise which had few internal safeguards and no external guarantees. The imperial drive to demolish the democratic principle guaranteed under the UN scheme, was backed by the larger imperialist design which sought to control Eritrean destiny. Clearly, the United Nations was not the forum for continuing the struggle. This was how the Eritrean Liberation Movement was born.

The Eritrean Liberation Movement
Clandestine Activities

The banning of labor union activities had sent the Eritrean labor movement underground. The ruthless and extensive use of police terror had also sent teachers, students, intellectuals, and other members of the Eritrean masses underground. The failure of peaceful petition, of the path of the law, created an atmosphere of siege which drove the Eritrean people to support the Eritrean resistance that came to be known as the Eritrean Liberation Movement (ELM).

The ELM had two principal centers: one situated in the highlands with its nucleus in Asmara, and the other in the lowlands with exiled Eritreans living in the Sudan providing inspiration. The two centers created various means of contact, including sports and other youth activities, but they were not organizationally linked. School teachers, students, intellectuals, and small tradesmen were the main recruits. Its organizational laxity and lack of a clear political program was its main handicap, which eventually led to its collapse, but not before it had prepared the ground for the next stage of struggle. Its highland version was known in its last phase as Mahber Shewate (the committee of seven), a cellular underground organization, organized in the urban centers. Its lowland version was known as Harakat' Atahrir Al Eritrea (The Eritrean Liberation Movement), or simply Haraka.

ELM in Disarray Due to Arrests and Police Terror

The United Nations arrangement had provided a modicum of democratic rights from which the Eritrean people tried to benefit. But we have seen that it was all to no avail. One of the most dramatic expressions of resistance through the exercise of such democratic rights was the general strike of the Eritrean labor unions noted above. The unions had been officially banned, but they continued to exist underground. The strike and the demonstrations which accompanied them were evidence of the

Eritrean national will to resist the demolition of democratic rights and to continue the struggle. Pitted against this national resistance was a determined imperial government which had US imperialism on its side and a mercenary Eritrean leadership and security machine at its command.

The ELM had made its presence felt in several ways. One of the most significant weapons was the pamphlet which was clandestinely produced and circulated, and was avidly sought and read. Another was the cultural medium. The Tigrigna language, which was banished from official function, was kept alive in debates in local clubs, schools, and theaters. Songs and poems came out in profusion and were heard in private homes, in cafes and restaurants, at weddings, funeral services, and during mourning. This defiance only served to harden the imperial line and tighten its security machine. Massive police raids and arrests left the movement decapitated, and on the run.

Fugitive Movement Transformed to Armed Struggle

The ELM had carried the national struggle one stage forward, despite its handicaps, and cleared the way for the only alternative left to the Eritrean people, that is, a protracted and popularly based armed struggle in the countryside. It is important to remember that the armed struggle was begun after the Eritrean people had tried all other possible means of resistance. This is an historical fact, in keeping with the Declaration of Human Rights which proclaimed that "it is essential if man is not to be compelled to have recourse, as a last resort, to rebellion against tyranny and oppression, that human rights should be protected by the rule of law."

Ethiopia's breach of its pledge to abide by the Declaration of Human Rights and its violation of the terms of the UN resolution thus led to armed struggle, as a last resort. The Eritrean Liberation Front (ELF) announced the beginning of the armed struggle in September 1961. War, it has been said, is the continuation of politics by other means. It is the hard way, and in the Eritrean case, it was the only way. What was left of the ELM (together with other elements) was driven to form the ELF.

Certain exiled Eritrean leaders, such as Idris Mohamed Adam, who had resigned from his position as president of the Eritrean Assembly; Ibrahim Sultan Ali, secretary general of the Islamic League Party (Rabita'l Islamia); and Wolde-Ab, leader of the Independence Party and (later) president of the Eritrean labor unions were involved. These exiled leaders lived in Cairo, from where they had made unsuccessful attempts to petition the UN. Even when they launched the ELF, some had hoped that the gunshots would draw the attention of the UN. This too proved a vain hope.

Idris and Ibrahim had visited Saudi Arabia earlier (in 1960) and made contacts with the Eritrean community there which called upon them to form an organization and start an armed struggle. Exiled Eritrean communities in other Arab countries and in particular an active student body in Cairo had also been making similar calls. Upon his return to Cairo, Idris announced the establishment of the ELF and was immediately beset with factional strife, principally originating from the foreign section of the ELM, which claimed prior legitimacy. It was amid such strife that Hamid Idris Awate, an Eritrean who had been an NCO in the Sudanese Army and a renowned "rebel" during British rule of Eritrea, announced the armed struggle from the western lowlands of Eritrea. The ELF foreign group led by Idris Mohamed Adam endorsed Idris Awate's declaration and decided to send him needed supplies.

Awate died in mid-1962 but the liberation army of the ELF continued to grow. Its guerilla army was led by Eritrean soldiers or NOCs in the Sudanese Army. By mid-1964, when the first foreign assistance came from Syria in the form of 20 Kalashnikov assault rifles, the guerilla army had grown to 250. By that time also young Eritreans from the highlands and from the urban centers of the Sudan and Egypt began to join. These were mostly students and workers. But the bulk of the guerila army was and remained for the next six or seven years made up of Eritreans from the rural and nomadic communities of the western lowlands. This imbalance left the students and workers from the cities in the minority, and was to become a serious point of contention in the following years.

The critical defect of the ELF was its lack of a clear political line and a disciplined organization following such a line. Very few meetings were held. A meeting held at Kassala in 1965 was called to divide the field into five military regions (like the Algerian willayas), each to be led by a virtually autonomous regional commander. The field division was done along ethnic, regional, and religious lines.

This political and organizational defect affected the life and progress of the guerilla army in the field. The division of the regions created intense rivalries, corruption of power, and tyranny. This led to the split of the progressive wing of the ELF to form the Eritrean People's Liberation Forces (EPLF), which in 1977 changed the word "forces" to front.

ANNEXATION

Circumstances Surrounding the Act of Annexation

National Resistance to Continued Violation of Law—
Activities of the ELF

Emperor Haile Selassie annexed Eritrea on November 14, 1962. As the foregoing discussion has shown, the Emperor had begun to carry out his annexationist plans long before the final act of abrogation abolishing the federation. The ELM must be seen as an expression of the Eritrean peoples' resistance, partly in response to such annexationist ambition and, of course, as a continuation of the struggle against colonial rule or foreign domination. The declaration of armed struggle in 1961 marked a definitive stage in that resistance and struggle.

Trevaskis, political secretary of the British administration in Eritrea, knew of Ethiopia's imperial ambitions. He wrote in his book:

> The temptation to subject Eritreans firmly under her control will always be great. Should she try to do so, she will risk Eritrean discontent and eventual revolt, which, with foreign sympathy and support, might well disrupt both Eritrea and Ethiopia herself.[29]

Trevaskis' prophecy was fulfilled. The Eritrean resistance struggle continued underground. The declaration of armed struggle only sharpened the conflict and aroused more people to intensify their resistance. One simple example will serve to illustrate the qualitative change in the underground resistance following annexation. Eritrean university students and other Eritreans residing in Ethiopia continued the clandestine activities under tighter cellular organizations. One group initiated the idea of an annual oratorical contest in the Tigrigna language to be conducted in Eritrea. The YMCA (Asmara Branch) provided the forum and other facilities. This contest annoyed the Ethiopian officials who were busy rooting out Tigrigna from official affairs. But there was a limit to the imperial fiat. And the importance of culture and language as a measure of resistance cannot be overemphasized.

Meanwhile the ELF, despite its internal contradictions, carried out strikes on selected targets in the lowlands. The deeds were reported immediately by word of mouth, thus reinforcing the spirit of resistance throughout Eritrea and among Eritreans in Ethiopia.

Tacit United States Support for Ethiopian Claims

Earlier discussions in this paper have demonstrated that the Ethiopian aim of annexing Eritrea was backed by the government of the United States of America. UN Resolution 390 A(v) itself was a compromise solution which fell short of Ethiopian demands and US backing, because of the divided views on the report of the Commission of Enquiry. The next best thing from the viewpoint of Ethiopia and its supporters was to devise a scheme covered up with legal cosmetics in order to meet objection and answer criticisms. Once the "federal" scheme was launched and US interests gained a foothold, events would take care of themselves.

The documents quoted and discussed in Section I.B. above provide some insight into the making of the strategy that would ultimately undo the UN resolution, itself a US-inspired contrivance designed as a stopgap to eventual annexation.

In terms of international politics, the American alliance with Ethiopia, which had manoeuvered the UN into sacrificing the Eritrean people, turned Ethiopia into an imperialist client state (or a neocolony). Haile Selassie's violation of the resolution was therefore tacitly supported by the US. The Eritrean struggle thus became at once an anti-colonial and anti-imperialist struggle.

John Spencer, the then American adviser to the Ethiopian government, has since sought to provide an ex post facto justification to the annexation, as follows:

> While deploring this action (annexation) both ethically and politically, the author must observe that it was not entirely without legal basis. Both the American and British members of the informal six-state drafting Committee... had particularly stressed to the Ethiopian Foreign Minister that acceptance by Ethiopia of the provision in the Federal Act (paragraph 13 of U.N. Resolution 390 A(V)) requiring its adoption by the Eritrean Assembly would thereby justify termination of the Federation upon a concurring vote of that Assembly, without need of approval by the U.N. General Assembly. In fact, in previous years, the Eritrean Assembly had voted resolutions similar to that adopted in 1962, which the Ethiopian government had refrained from invoking.[30]

The absurdity of this opinion is too obvious to merit any serious discussion. Actually it gives the game away, adding further evidence of US complicity in the annexation which in turn explains the silence of the UN. It is enough to refer to the opinion of the panel of jurists cited in Matienzo's final report quoted above, by way of rebuttal.[31] Spencer also conveniently ignored the terms of the whole federal arrangement, including the Eritrean constitution. Article 91 of that constitution, entitled "Compliance with the Federal Act and the principles of democratic government," provides:

1. The Assembly may not, by means of an amendment, introduce into the constitution any provision which would not be in conformity with the Federal Act.
2. Article 16 of the Constitution, by the terms of which the Constitution of Eritrea is based on the principles of democratic government, shall not be amended.

If amendment of Article 16 is precluded, then *a fortiori* abrogation of the whole structure is null and void.

Ethiopian Campaign of Bribery

The imperial Ethiopian government had used the Unionist party as a rubber stamp to advance its annexationist aims as early as the 1940s. Even in those years, when the imperial design had not yet completely revealed its true nature, there was no popular basis for Ethiopia's claim. As Trevaskis has written, there was no "spontaneous demonstration of pro-Ethiopian feelings in Eritrea... If they were not to lose their case by default, the Ethiopians had to arouse some Eritrean support."[32] To that end the imperial government had turned first to the higher clergy of the Coptic church which had been dispossessed by the Italians. With promises of land and other privileges the high clergy had become ready tools for the annexationist designs. The Coptic church threatened excommunication, refused baptismal rites, and funeral and other religious services for all Christian Eritreans who were opposed to the annexation designs. One of the architects of the abrogation of the federation was Dimetros, the most influential Coptic cleric in Eritrea, who was also the vice-president—and *eminence grise* (gray eminence)—of the Eritrean Assembly.

Next to the high clergy of the Coptic church came the higher echelons of the urban petty bourgeoisie, and some members of the intelligentsia recruited with rewards of office and material benefits. To this class of Eritreans was added a few of the leading feudal elements from the western parts of Eritrea, who faced revolts of their serfs. These were not only bribed into joining the Unionist camp but were encouraged to stand election for membership to the Eritrean Assembly.

Finally, the patriotic elements who refused to be bribed were later given various sinecure appointments or otherwise comfortably settled. The emperor's representative, the chief executive and the vice-president of the assembly were busy summoning people individually and in groups. There are unconfirmed stories of cash transactions "under the table" during the days preceding the "vote."

The Event of Annexation
Ethiopian Troop Movements—An Atmosphere of Siege

Ethiopian (federal) jurisdiction, under the UN arrangements, included defense. Under the pretext of that jurisdiction imperial forces were dispatched and spread over large areas of Eritrea as part of the strategy of annexation. The large presence of the imperial forces in Eritrean urban centers, especially Asmara, the capital, added both to the heightened sense of siege to which Eritreans were subjected.

Actually the imperial strategists need not have bothered to add the imperial forces. For, in addition to bribery, the Eritrean police, under the autocratic command of their chief, had done most of the intimidation needed to secure the requisite "votes." But the imperial strategists wanted to make assurance doubly sure. They did not trust the Eritrean police even as commanded by their henchman. Thus the police which held the Eritrean Assembly virtually under siege was itself under siege by a larger and better-armed Ethiopian army.

Police Terror and a "Legislative Act" at Gunpoint

Richard Greenfield has asserted in a book published a little over two years after the annexation, that there was no vote taken in the Eritrean Assembly, and that instead the Eritrean Chief Executive (a hired hand) simply read a prepared statement. Greenfield, who was a close observer of the scene at the time, suggests that no vote had ever been taken.[33] He has recently reiterated this, adding that his assertion has not been contested.

But even if there had been voting, it would still be null and void due to the absence of an essential legislative precondition: freedom to exercise the voting right voluntarily. Long before "voting" day, several of the patriotic members of the Assembly known for their independent leanings, were subjected to police harassment. Some were even arrested and beaten up. Others were forcibly brought to the assembly following a period in which they were absent from the assembly. It is irresistable, at this point, to note similar conditions in Namibia controlled by South African authorities in 1978—a development aptly caricatured as "Vote or I will shoot." The Eritrean Assembly was itself filled with police armed with machine guns and placed at strategic positions visible to "voting" members of the assembly.

Meanwhile, the final legal package for the imperial strategists had been prepared well in advance. A proclamation announcing the "Termination of the Federal Status of Eritrea and the Application to Eritrea of the System of Unitary Administration of the Empire of Ethiopia . . . " was issued. That was the title under which Order No. 27 of 1962 was promulgated the day after the "voting" was supposed to have taken place. It was the hour of triumph for imperial strategy. Order No. 27 had been prepared by John Spencer months ahead of time. The preamble shows the "lawmaker" grappling with the question of how to package and present in a more favorable light the naked act of aggression. Listen, for example, to the following tongue-in-cheek statement:

> . . . Whereas, the people of Eritrea have come progressively to realize the disadvantages flowing from the federal system of administration and have increasingly and repeatedly requested the abolition of this system, which they have never sought . . . Now, therefore, . . . we hereby order as follows . . .

Then the final *coup de grace* of Article 2:

> The Federal status of Eritrea and Ethiopia is hereby terminated and Eritrea, which continues to constitute an integral part of the Empire of Ethiopia, is hereby wholly integrated into the unitary system of administration of Our Empire.

And Article 3 rationalizes the historic retrogression of a democratic system taken over by imperial autocracy. It provides:

> The Revised Constitution of Ethiopia given by Us as the Sovereign and Crown of the Empire of Ethiopia on November 2, 1955, shall continue to be the sole and exclusive Constitution to apply uniformly throughout the territory of the Empire of Ethiopia.

Indeed the Revised Constitution of 1955 was "given" by the emperor with annexation of Eritrea in mind, to put forward a "democratic" face.

The only true words in all of this legal packaging are those in the quoted preamble which state that the Eritrean people never sought the federal system. They sought independence, as they always have and always will until final victory. The use of the words "which continues to constitute an integral part," in Article 2, and "shall continue to be the sole and exclusive constitution" in Article 3 indicates that the imperial government had never accepted (and hence never complied with) the internationally arranged federation. This adds to the mountain of evidence proving that the Ethiopian government did not comply with the terms and conditions of the UN resolution.

CONCLUSION: ERITREA IS UNIQUELY A UN RESPONSIBILITY

We have seen that the Eritrean armed struggle was a last resort measure taken in the face of UN failure to sanction Ethiopian violation of the terms and conditions of the UN resolution. Such failure becomes easy to understand in view of the more fundamental failure of the UN in the first place: the failure to recognize the right of the Eritrean people to self-determination. That basic failure was followed by a failure to provide clear and adequate remedies in the event of violation of the terms and conditions of the resolution and laws based upon it. The ambiguity of the legal status of Eritrea in international law, and the absence of remedies facilitated the process of continued violation and eventual annexation.

Finally, the UN failed miserably when Emperor Haile Selassie abolished with impunity its own imposed federation. In terms of international law, the emperor's violation of the terms of the UN resolution from the very first moment constituted an illegal act which should have caused the General Assembly to be "seized of jurisdiction," as Matienzo had reported. Repeated pleas by Eritreans made to the UN went unheeded. When the imperial aim of final annexation became increasingly clear the Eritrean resistance took a more militant form. Legally, the violation of the terms of the UN resolution as an international instrument, and the silent complicity of the UN, gave the Eritrean people the additional right to wage a struggle for national self-determination and independence.

After the Ethiopian imperial regime had by its own acts become an illegal, occupationist colonial regime, the duty of the UN was to sanction the illegal acts and apply the principle of self-determination. Such failure placed the Eritrean people to the *status quo ante* (to pre-September 1950) in which the Eritrean people were once more a people struggling against colonial rule and/or alien domination. That is why the Eritrean question is a colonial question, and not one of secession.

The abolition of the federation was the climax of a series of illegal acts. It constituted an illegal act in the eyes of the law because:

1. the Eritrean Assembly was made to act under duress;
2. even without such duress the Assembly had no legal right to abolish the federation;

3. as a creation of international law the federation could only be abolished by an international legal instrument.

The federation of Eritrea with Ethiopia was a unique UN device dictated by imperialist strategic and geopolitical interests. Even so, a flagrant violation of the terms of the federation should never have gone unsanctioned. Indeed the correct and just step to take would have been to give the Eritreans the free choice to determine their future. But even in a less clear case—when there is no unique UN responsibility—the illegal seizure by a powerful state of a non-self-governing territory should not pass unsanctioned.

In this respect UN Resolutions 1514 (xv) and 1541 (xv) are relevant. According to these resolutions the future of a non-self-governing territory may be determined in one of three ways:

1. emergence as a sovereign independent state;
2. free association with an independent state;
3. integration with an independent state.

The implementation of any of these options requires free voluntary and informed choice arrived at through democratic processes. Whether it is free association or integration, the process should involve the free and democratic expression of the will of the people involved "impartially conducted and based on universal adult suffrage. The United Nations could, when it deems it necessary, supervise these processes."

Thus, over and above the universal principle of self-determiantion discussed in the first part of this paper, the case of Eritrea merits special consideration. The unsanctioned illegal acts of the imperial Ethiopian government lends the Eritrean struggle a more specific legitimacy under international law. The UN, having failed to honor its own resolution, had implicitly recognized the right of the Eritrean people to wage their struggle in the only way possible. The UN is now—and has been since the beginning of the violation—under obligation to translate the legitimacy of the Eritrean people's struggle to practical legality. To be more precise, the UN must openly and emphatically recognize its past failure and recognize the right of the Eritrean people to self-determination and independence. There can be no reversion to "federation."

NOTES

1. See for example a Top Secret Memorandum of March 5, 1949, written with the UN Third Session in view, from Mr. Rusk to the Secretary of State.
2. See *United Nations Yearbook*, 1948-49, pp. 256-279.
3. See Resolution 289 A(iv).
4. *Ibid.*
5. Letter written December 11, 1948.
6. Department of State, Memorandum of Conversation, March 30, 1949.
7. See, for example, a Secret Internal Memo of September 27, 1948.
8. *Ibid.*
9. Department of State, Incoming Telegram, received August 22, 1949, from Addis Ababa, signed MERREL, to Secretary of State, No. 171, August 19, 1949.
10. *Ibid.*
11. G.K.N. Trevaskis, *Eritrea: A Colony in Transition* (Greenwood, 1975), p. 74.
12. *Ibid.*
13. In a statement before the commission set up to investigate Haile Selassie's government, August 1974.
14. See text of the Agreement between Ethiopia and the United States concerning the American Base in Eritrea, signed on May 22, 1953.
15. See, for example, Articles VII, XVII, XVIII, XIX(3).
16. Quoted in Linda Heiden, *The Eritrean Struggle for Independence*, Monthly Review, 30.2 (June 1978):15.
17. See Sir W. Ivor Jennings, *The Approach to Self-Government* (Cambridge University Press, 1956).
18. *Ibid.*, p. 21.
19. *Final Report to the United Nations Commissioner to Eritrea*, Chapter II, para. 201.
20. Alain Fenet in Alain Fenet, Cao-Huy-Thuan, and Tran-Van-Minh, *La Question de l'Erythrée* (Paris: Presses Universitaires de France, 1979), p. 22.
21. cf. *ibid.*, p. 24.
22. Eritrean Constitution, Article 5.
23. *Ibid.*, Article 12.
24. *Ibid.*, Article 18.
25. *Ibid.*, Article 19.
26. *Ibid.*, Articles 22-34.
27. See Article 91(2).
28. As reported to the author by Tsegay Iyassu, a prominent Eritrean lawyer and scholar who witnessed events in Eritrea in those years and thereafter.
29. See G.H.N. Trevaskis, op cit.
30. John H. Spencer, *Ethiopia: The Horn of African and U.S. Policy* (Washington, D.C., 1977), p. 31, footnote 68.
31. See footnote 19 above.
32. Trevaskis, op. cit., p. 59.

Chapter 3
*Evolution of the Principle of Self-Determination**

GENERAL AND HISTORICAL

The idea of self-determination has played a central role in the emancipation of humanity from different forms of oppression. The conditions under which it has been invoked as a mediating principle have differed. But in all cases, the common denominator has been one oppressive nation or class that dominates another.

The idea gained international recognition in modern times during the peace-making process of 1918-19 at Versailles. Woodrow Wilson proclaimed it "an imperative principle of action," adding an injunction that statesmen would "henceforth ignore it at their peril." However, there was no universal agreement even within the domestic policy of the same nation as can be shown by the lamentation of Robert Lansing, Wilson's Secretary of State, who wrote: "the phrase is simply loaded with dynamite. It will raise hopes which can never be realized. It will, I fear, cost thousands of lives. In the end it is bound to be distorted, to be called the dream of an idealist who failed to realize the danger until too late, to check those who attempt to put the principle in force. What a calamity the phrase was ever uttered. What misery it will cause."[1]

---

*This paper was originally presented at the African Studies Association Conference in Baltimore, Maryland on November 4, 1978.

Lansing's view evidently lacks historical perspective. It is as single-mindedly pro status quo as Wilson's is passionately idealistic. Why was Lansing so fearful about the "danger" of "those who attempt to put the principle in force"? Or, more pertinently, why would there be such people in the first place? As it happened, Lansing's fears proved to be a self-fulfilling prophecy, as nations which had been part of the empires—Austro-Hungarian in Europe, Turkish in the Middle East—began to demand self-government in the name of a principle proclaimed by the victorious allies of the war.

It must be remembered that the principle of self-determination as proclaimed in 1918 was powerfully backed by the events in Russia when the revolution abolished a feudal autocracy, ushering in a new era for the oppressed Russian masses. The Wilsonian ideal was therefore ironically enough supported by the Leninist principle of self-determination, which was eventually enshrined in the constitution of the USSR.

Nor was Lenin the first to deal with self-determination in socialist writings. For example, commenting on the checkered history of oppression and struggle of the people of Poland, Frederick Engels wrote in 1892:

> The restoration of an independent strong Poland is a matter which concerns not only the Poles but all of us. A sincere international collaboration of the European nations is possible only if each of these nations is fully autonomous in its own house. The revolution of 1848 which under the banner of the proletariat, after all, merely let the proletarian fighters do the work of the bourgeoisie, also secured the independence of Italy, Germany, and Hungary through its testamentary executors, Louis Bonaparte and Bismarck; but Poland, which since 1792 had done more for the revolution than all those three put together, was left to its own resources, when it succumbed in 1863 to tenfold greater Russian force. The nobility could neither maintain nor refrain Polish independence; today to the bourgeoisie, this independence is, to say the least, immaterial. It can be gained only by the young proletariat, and in its hands it is safe.[2]

Historically, we find this idea of self-determination invoked in two types of situations which often overlap: an oppressed or colonized nation claiming and fighting for its national independence and, at another level, an oppressed class. Examples of both will be adduced in later sections. In this section I will make an attempt to go beyond the modern historical context to examine the basis or source of the idea of self-determination, which becomes inchoate the further away one travels in historical time.

To the discerning observer of the modern phenomenon of nationalism, it is clear that a deep-seated emotional appeal lies in the very concept of the nation which generations of nationalist leaders have used as a crystallizing center for grievances felt against alien rule. This is particularly true in the colonial experience, in which nationalist leaders used nationalism as a powerful rallying force first to question the legitimacy of an alien ruler and second to unite societies disintegrating under the impact of colonial rule by offering a national program of action in which—on paper at any rate—the people would perform as principal actors in fashioning their own destiny.

What then lies behind the doctrine of self-determination in the name of which nations have won their freedom? In the continuing debate on the "inner contents" of self-determination, those who argue on the side of the status quo summon to their aid "law and order" or "good government and efficient administration," or "national unity and territorial integrity." Their ideologues are quick to point out the "relativity of political principles" in order to deny the demand of self-government made in the name of self-determination.

Although it is customary to trace self-determination as a modern political principle to 17th- and 18th-century demands for government by consent, it is argued that the concept is rooted in man's moral feelings, and as such goes far beyond the 17th or 18th century. Probing the origins of such moral feelings, Joan Robinson, for example, has argued that it can be traced to primordial biological needs.

> The biological necessity for morality arises, because for the species to survive, any animal must have on the one hand some egoism—a strong urge to get food for himself and to defend his means of livelihood; also—extending egoism from the individual to the family—to fight for the interests of his mate and his young. On the other hand, social life is impossible unless the pursuit of self-interest is mitigated by respect and compassion for others.[3]

Morality is portrayed here as a necessary principle of reciprocal action—something that is desired and upheld for its own sake. The moral imperative, in other words, is based on a social imperative. Religion was added not as an inseparable part, but as a sort of insurance scheme to back it up. Morality does not necessarily derive from religion. Consequently, those who have no religious beliefs are inclined to try to derive moral feelings from other sources, such as reason. But moral feelings are not derived from reason, although it may not always be easy to disentangle the two. Rather, like the faculty of speech, moral feelings are a separate feature of the human armory.

Then there is ideology, which as a basis of social action may encompass both religion and reason, depending on the stage of development of the society. From the standpoint of evolution, Joan Robinson postulates that ideology acts as a higher substitute for instinct. "Animals seem to know what to do; we have to be taught."[4] In the dynamics of human and social life there is interaction between reason, ideology, morality, and religion, where it is applicable. And language or speech acts as common denominator. Language, indeed, at times so colors the thinking process that words assume an authority of their own. It was in this sense that Disraeli uttered his famous dictum: "It is with words that we govern men." Speech is, as Whorf puts it, "the best show man puts on . . . It is his own particular act on the stage of evolution, in which he comes before the cosmic backdrop."[5]

Words, especially when they represent important concepts, become so charged with symbolic significance that they govern people's conduct. Self-determination has assumed such significance.

The primary factor underlying the concept is physical survival, as the first law of nature. From the physical survival of the individual and his immediate group to a larger association of people held by common historical and cultural bonds, the principle of survival has been rationalized with appropriate rituals centered around vital resources. In the face of any threat to the survival of a group, the response is group solidarity. Such solidarity is interwoven in the social fabric and made binding by rituals and laws. This may be summed up as the ideology of a given society.

The threat that any given society faces more often than not takes the form of competition for the control of vital resources, and wars have been fought over such issues throughout history. In the African pre-colonial historical experience, empires have arisen and expanded by conquering smaller nations and appropriating their resources. By and large, however, and in the absence of empires, the predatory urge seems to have been harnessed in (inter-national) (or inter-tribal) cooperation consummated by participation in each other's rituals—which meant a symbiosis of two or more ideologies in a "peaceful coexistence," to use a modern term.

The intrusion of colonial adventure meant among other things, a disturbance of such balance of interests. There was no higher law to which the colonized peoples could appeal in the face of an alien conquest. As international law and morality evolved between and among the colonizing nations, those of the colonized peoples exposed to western education silently observed their application(s). And they saw that international law rationalized the will of the victorious. The idea of self-determination began to gain potency only when the mighty began to indulge in self-doubt in the inter-war years (1919-1939).

The principle of self-determination was derived from a set of old doctrines, the most important of which is the proposition that government must rest on the consent of the governed. But as Rupert Emerson has pointed out, the nineteenth and twentieth centuries "added the assumption that, since man is a *national animal*, the government to which he will give this consent is one representing his own nation."[6] The old claim that individuals must consent to or contractually establish the governments ruling them is "thus transmitted into the natural right of nations to determine their own statehood."[7] Thomas Hodgkin links the rise of African nationalism in a similar fashion: "the rise of African nationalism is thought of as the final stage in a chain-reaction, deriving its operative ideas originally from the French revolution—the doctrine of the Rights of Man interpreted as the Rights of Nations."[8]

The colonial adventure legitimized in the Berlin Treaty of 1885 was questioned as the colonial powers—twice victorious allies in two world wars—began to lose faith in themselves. As a parallel development, the force of nationalism as a univeral political phenomenon began to compel attention. The emphasis given to the right of small nations in the 1918-1919 negotiation focussed in Europe eventually expanded to engulf the whole world. The covenant of the League of Nations which came out of those negotiations had left the colonies under the European imperial system and the US colony of the Philippines out of its considerations, to the discretion of the colonial powers. But the promulgation of self-determination as a guiding principle had revolutionary implications, as the tidal wave of nationalist movements would demonstrate. The attack against colonialism as an imperial system gathered momentum in the inter-war years.[9] It was utterly discredited by the end of World War II. With the creation of the United Nations and the incorporation in the Charter of the United Nations of self-determination as a universally accepted principle, colonialism as imperial system came to an end. But the application of self-determiantion as a right—as compared to its proclamation as a guiding principle—has been problematic.

SELF-DETERMINATION IN THE POST-COLONIAL ERA

Europe's colonization of the world is often regarded as coterminous with the birth of the modern world. This view gives colonialism a historical justification by which nationalism and self-determination are adopted as its offspring. Nationalism, to be sure, emerged as a reaction to the colonial experience, and nationalist leaders as the educational products of its "modernizing process." But the colonized peoples generally do not remember colonialism with gratitude, even though they have not been able or willing to reorder its historical consequences.

In this latter sense nationalism may be regarded as a child of colonialism. It may also be so regarded in a more restrictive, territorial sense, when defined in terms of the colonial borders created for the administrative convenience of an exploitative imperial system, in reckless disregard of the fates of divided peoples. The patchwork quilt presented by the political map of Africa readily attests to that.

But nationalism is also a reclamation of a natural urge to recreate an image of a community with which man as a social animal needs to identify. The resugence of ethnicity in the United States of America in the early 1970s indicates the deep-seated nature of such urges, even in a country where the capitalist "melting pot" has been at work for two centuries.[10] As the American anthropologist, Wilton Dillon, has observed:

> On the threshold of our 200th anniversary as a republic the United States still is in search of a philosophy or a rationale for that web of human behaviour we abstractly call "diversity," "dissent," "deviation," or "pluralism," and is seeking how to reconcile that search with the political demands of "solidarity," "loyalty," and "security" as perceived by persons temporarily in power.[11]

The United Nations has played a crucial role as a forum for the articulation of nationalist aspirations for self-determination. Such articulation has been necessarily anti-colonialist and anti-imperialist. No one openly defended colonialism as an imperial system, even though rearguard actions persisted into the 1970s. The conversion of the British empire into the "Commonwealth of Nations," and the proclamation of the Guallist communauté in 1958 are the best examples of such rearguard actions. The role of the United States as a senior partner of the NATO alliance with colonial powers as its junior partners, belied its professed anti-colonial aims.

For the colonial powers self-determination for the colonized was synonymous with self-destruction of imperial interests. It is a measure of the irresistible force of nationalist independence movements that the imperial powers openly advocated and endorsed self-determination as a universal principle in 1945, even though they knew that it was a weapon aimed primarily at themselves. It did not mean, however, that they were ready to wind up their business and go home. The French waged colonial wars in Algeria, in Indochina until the disaster at Dienbienphou, and elsewhere. The British, who were more pragmatic, refined their neocolonial instruments. Even as Churchill echoed Disraeli's imperial dream—"I did not become Her Majesty's Prime Minister to preside over the liquidation of the British Empire"—the colonial bureaucrats and their masterminds at Whitehall were busy designing a future "Commonwealth of Nations" in which physical, military occupation was gradually replaced by economic remote control.

The nationalist leaders who had been called a "band of agitators" all of a sudden became responsible leaders. As early as 1938, some farsighted colonial policymakers were looking ahead preparing a transfer of power to a safe native "elite."[12] Not all of them turned out to be "safe." Some even "agitated" for the liquidation of empires forthwith. Nkrumah's conception of Pan-Africanism, for instance, and his initiatives to call an All-African Heads of States meeting in 1958 followed by an All-African People's Conference in 1958-59 was aimed at the liquidation of the remaining vestiges of colonialism in Africa. He also sought an "African socialist reconstruction," thus giving self-determination a new meaning. He wrote:

> We postulate each man to be an end in himself, not merely a means; and we accept the necessity of guaranteeing each man equal opportunities for his development. The implications of this for sociopolitical practice have to be worked out scientifically, and the necessary social and economic politics pursued with resolution.[13]

It is also worth noting that one of the mottos of Nkrumah's party (the CPP) was: "We prefer self-government with danger than servitude in tranquility." But the silent war goes on as neocolonialism's subtle designs for development continue to define "basic human needs."

The United Nations Charter has placed self-determination on a pedestal as a universal principle. But the application of the principle has turned out to be highly problematic in a colonially established post-colonial legal order. The earlier version of the charter (the Dumbarton Oaks version) made no mention of self-determination. But at San Francisco the four sponsoring governments introduced it at the suggestion of the Soviet Union. The final version is found in Articles 1 and 55 of the charter. The relevant clauses read as follows:

> *Article 1(2):* [the purposes of the United Nations are]
> to develop friendly relations among nations based on respect for the principle of equal rights and self-determination of peoples, and to take other appropriate measures to strengthen universal peace...
> *Article 55:*
> With a view to the creation of conditions of stability and well-being which are necessary for peaceful and friendly relations among

nations based on respect for the principle of equal rights and self-determination of people, the United Nations shall promote:
   (a) higher standards of living, full employment, and conditions of economic and social progress and development:
   (b) solutions of international economic, social, health and related problems; and international cultural and educational cooperation; and
   (c) universal respect for, and observance of, human rights and fundamental freedoms for all without distinction as to race, sex, language or religion.

Two basic aspects of self-determination emerge from this: one which is traditionally political, involving nations or peoples; and another which is economic. The advent and progress of these two aspects have continued to grow with the evolution of the international community since 1945.

POLITICAL SELF-DETERMINATION SINCE 1945

The nations of the Third World have shown a remarkable degree of unity in their common goal of *economic* self-determination. But there has not been a similar unity of views or positions when it comes to *political* self-determination. The reason may be historical or it may have to do with the political complexity of a polarized world, in which the Third World tries to be nonaligned but cannot. In most instances colonial, territorial heritage is the root of the problem—Africa's "problems of nationalities." The African states are caught between two conflicting claims: the political imperative of stability and nation-building on the one hand, and the moral/philosophical imperative of self-determination as a universally accepted principle to which they themselves appealed during their struggle for freedom.

Nor is this crisis of conflicting values limited to Africa or other parts of the Third World. With varying degrees of intense feelings and organized militance, it exists in a number of countries—from Ireland to Belgium in Europe, to Quebec in Canada, and Puerto Rico in the United States. Welsh and Scottish nationalism has risen to the point where British Parliament has been spending more time debating their future in the British constitutional set-up.

The situation in the Soviet Union—the principal supporter of anti-colonial movements—is even more interesting. There, the Leninist principle of self-determination which involves a right of secession is incorporated into the constitution of the USSR. No one could therefore level a charge of hypocrisy at the Soviet Union when it was advocating and actively supporting other peoples' demands for self-determination. It is quite another matter to raise the question whether the Soviet Union will in practice permit the exercise of the right to self-determination "up to and including secession" (to use Lenin's terms).

But recent events in the Horn of Africa have proved that the Soviet Union is not immune to charges of inconsistency or duplicity. In 1950, when the future of the ex-Italian colonies was being debated, the Soviet Union supported the legitimate rights of the Eritrean people to complete independence, whereas the Western powers led by the United States sacrificed the Eritrean people (and with them the principle of self-determination) on the altar of power politics. Yet in 1977 the Soviet Union reversed its position for political, strategic considerations. The legitimate struggle for independence now became unacceptable "secession" which had acquired a negative significance.

Reactions to this reversal range from denunciations of "opportunism" to "dialectical" analyses in which the Soviet view of self-determination is explained as being in consonance with revolutionary strategies. Self-determination is acceptable where it is applied to break imperial structures, but it is not where it hurts a socialist country, especially the USSR. This seems to be the argument advanced in the Eritrean case. But there is at least one difficulty: who decides who is more socialist than whom? The arrogation of the right to decide that question is itself palpably anti-democratic which strikes at the root of self-determination as a principle.

The Eritrean independence struggle which is now in its 18th year has passed through various revolutionary phases. In its present stage and particularly as led by the EPLF (Eritrean People's Liberation Front) it is more authentically socialist than any military government can ever hope to be, even as it proclaims Marxist-Leninist slogans, which is what the Dergue (the Ethiopian military governments central committee) has been doing. In the face of these incontrovertible facts, the Soviet Union at the very least would be perpetrating a fraud if it were to cause the denial of freedom to the Eritreans.

The Soviet Union is not alone today in facing the dilemma posed by demands for self-determination. In point of historical fact, the United States and Britain as imperial powers have ridden roughshod over it. Self-determination has often become, as Emerson put it, "a right to be defended in lofty terms when it is politically advantageous and to be rejected when it is not... The Soviet Union finds it an excellent right for use against the West and its colonies as the West holds it eminently applicable to the peoples of the U.S.S.R. and its satellites."[14] The Soviet support of India in the

India-Pakistan war which led to the birth of Bangladesh through East Pakistan's secession is cited as an example of the support of self-determination as strategically or politically motivated. But in that instance at least the action is consistent with the traditional Soviet position on self-determination.

The blemished record of the Western powers is nowhere more blemished than in southern Africa. Suffice it to say that from their support of Portuguese colonial wars against the peoples of Angola, Guinea-Bissau, and Mozambique to their complicity in Zimbabwe (in some cases) and in South Africa (in all cases); they have done violence to a principle to which they gave their solemn endorsement.

As for the independent African governments, it must be said, in fairness to them, that they inherited the problem associated with the demand for the exercise of the right to self-determination. But they also inherited state power of no mean import. That power, which many in their governments have used to amass wealth and privilege, carries with it proportionate responsibility. One leader, the late Nkrumah, had offered an alternative to division of mini-states involved in mini-wars and disputes. He offered Pan-Africanism and expended his energies, talents, and considerable resources toward its achievement.

What happened in Cairo in 1964 at the second annual meeting of the heads of states and governments of the OAU put to rest (temporarily, one hopes) Nkrumah's dream. In response to perceived "problems of secession" the African leaders sanctified the colonial boundaries as the basis of defining African sovereign statehood. Somalia and Morocco walked out of that conference, reserving their right to continue to claim self-determination for the Ogaden in the case of Somalia, and for Mauritania in the case of Morocco. Morocco has since renounced its claim whereas the Ogaden has become a symbol of the blind alley that the international community has entered in relation to self-determination.

The United Nations as custodian of the principle carries the responsibility of providing an answer to this burning issue. Can there be an answer? One of the discerning students of the subject, Rupert Emerson, has suggested that self-determination is "essentially miscast in the role of a legal right which can be made an operative part of either [a] domestic or international system." Yet he recognizes it as a tremendous force which has already brough immense changes and predicts that it will continue to do so "as long as there are nations born and yet unborn (which) feel their destiny incomplete."[15] On the other hand he estimates that its revolutionary implications will keep it outside the constitutional framework. In this respect, the example (and future development) of the Soviet constitutional structure should provide an interesting lesson.

ECONOMIC SELF-DETERMINATION

In past centuries economic self-determination has been sought by oppressed and exploited peoples for an equitable share of the income of society, at first generally by supplications or petitions, but eventually taking the form of organized and militant demands. Concessions were made in the name of the "enlightened self-interest" of the propertied classes. The latest version of such concessions has been systematized in "social contracts" between labor and capital, with government acting as mediator. The emergence of inflation as an economic phenomenon has rendered labor captive to the system.

In the international domain, the division between industrialized capitalist nations and the underdeveloped peripheral nations is a function of the international economic order drawn up by the rich nations at the close of World War II in which poverty and affluence are linked in a causal relationship. The system is rooted in a powerful capitalist industrial machine, which is the result of a historical process including the colonial period. A dependence relationship was forcibly created by the capitalist nations which imposed their economy upon defenseless nations.

The end of the colonial era did not mean the end of exploitation and dependence. While political independence was achieved after a great deal of struggle, it was not accompanied by economic independence. The former colonial territories of the Third World remained economically weak and dependent on the former colonial powers and on the United States of America. Moreover, their dependence was (and is) critically linked with their underdevelopment, for the structure of dependence has led to unequal development—high rate of growth in the industrialized countries and very slow or no development in the rest. The gap between the two worlds grew wider, and the industrialized world enjoyed unprecedented growth in the quarter-century ending around 1973.

In the context of such a gap, economic self-determination expresses itself at two levels: at a theoretical level and at a political, organizational level. Theoretically, the Third World has begun to reject theories of economic development imposed by the West. Among the best known, earliest post-World War II writings on economic development is the book by W.W. Rostow. The underlying basis of Rostow's growth theory and that of most Western analysis is the historical experience of the industrialized capitalist world with its cultural values, interests, and ideologies. In sum, such theories placed great expectations on the monotized market economy of the underdeveloped countries—the sector critically linked with the capitalist economy—to absorb the traditional sector, with benefits expected to "trickle down" from the center to the periphery of these economies. It did not work out that way. Just as the gap grew larger between "rich and poor" nations, the few rich in the poor countries grew richer at the expense of the poor.

The industrialized countries have been developing their local counterparts or agents over this period and in some cases long before the end of the colonial era. The process involved education, the aggressive implanting and development of the market economy, and an aggressive new bourgeoisie owning (or part-owning) and managing a private sector. The evolving strategy involves what has been euphemistically called an international division of labor in which top management is recruited from the metropolitan "mother-companies" of what has now been named "multinational corporations," while workers are recruited from the local periphery countries at low wages. With this goes access to and control of raw materials and markets, facilitated by pre-existing colonial patterns of dependence.[16]

Thus the industrialized center insinuates itself (in contrast to the physical or military occupation of former days) with the economic and financial domain of a politically independent country in a bewildering variety of ways which are centrally planned and directed. It sells an enormous variety of goods and services as an organized irresistible economic force throughout the underdeveloped world. The goods all too often include luxury items as well as inappropriate technological products, which keep adding to a growing external debt burden and thus drain meagre foreign exchange reserves.

The ideological and political implications of such a powerful and wasteful economic presence are clear. It manifests itself in educational curricula, and in the whole communication system of the "poor" countries. All of this has been reproduced in the peripheral countries following the model of the "rich" countries. Economic self-determination at a theoretical level means a correct and relentless analysis of these phenomena and in proposing alternative models. There have been several such analyses and proposals in the past decade. Their central feature is self-reliance and a break with dependency.[17]

At the political/organizational level, economic self-determination has of course drawn heavily on the theoretical work, just as the revolutionaries of the 17th and 18th centuries used the philosophers and political theorists of their period. The challenge had been coming in one way or another since the time of the Bandung Conference in 1955, where the concept of non-alignment was first fashioned. Bandung was followed by the conference in Belgrade in 1961, which formally adopted "nonalignment" as an operative principle of action for the Third World. Similar conferences were held in Cairo (1964), Lusaka and Algiers (1973), Colombo (1976), Havana (1979), New Delhi (1983) and Harare (1986).[18]

In the economic sphere the Third World pushed for the establishment of the United Nations Conference on Trade and Development (UNCTAD), founded in 1964 under the leadership of Raul Prebisch, a prominent Argentinian economist and a leading member of the "dependencia theorists." UNCTAD provided the Third World a forum to express more systematically their growing dissatisfaction with the existing economic order. UNCTAD and the political side of the Non-Alignment Conferences reinforced each other. But it was at the UNCTAD conferences that the Third World clarified the issues of dependence under an unjust economic order. From UNCTAD I (1964) through UNCTAD II (1968) to UNCTAD III (1972), a more united Third World emerged with concrete demands for a just international order.

Between 1963 and 1973 several efforts were made to persuade the industrialized countries to grant better terms to Third World exporters of manufactured and processed goods—lower levels of import duties and fewer quota restrictions and non-tariff barriers than were imposed on imports from developed countries.[19] More important, the Third World's demand to improve their position in world trade was centered around commodity agreements, which has been consistently rejected by the industrialized countries.

By the time of UNCTAD III, the patience of the Third World was nearly exhausted under the increasing strain of trading and economic problems and a deteriorating international financial situation. When the Third World countries met in Algiers in 1973, the division between "North" and "South" had become clearcut, taking the form of a confrontation. The Third World for the time presented (at Algiers) the clearest, most coherent and comprehensive demand in the economic field. That demand was backed by a fortuitous event—the Yom Kipur war of 1973—which rallied Arab oil power behind the Third World, reflecting anger at America and the European countries which had supported Israel. Not only the Arab oil-producing countries but the whole of OPEC (Organization of Petroleum Exporting Countries), was as behind the new demand.

These events produced their own momentum. The powerful industrialized nations became aware of the limitations of their power. The Third World's perception of its new-found power included an awareness of the other side's growing restraint in the use of naked force to settle international issues of conflict. Kissinger's threat to use naked force in the wake of OPEC's action in 1973 did not impress the Third World.

Meanwhile the Third World took the initiative for the first itme in the United Nations' history of convening a special session of the General Assembly following the conclusion of the Algiers Conference. The Sixth Special Session of the UN was held from April 9 to May 2, 1974 to consider principles of governing a new international economic order. Algerian president Houari Boumedienne, speaking on behalf of the Third World, asserted that the time had come to change the old principles of international law in view of new developments in the world and "on the basis of the natural law of peoples to have what belongs to them and to deal with it as they saw fit, without being penalized for it, by paying a price to the very parties that had plundered and exploited them." "The international economic order," he went on, "is as unjust and as outmoded as the colonial order from which it draws sustenance." The Sixth Special Session of the General Assembly passed a resolution substantially adopting new principles for a new international economic order on the basis of the Third World demand.

The major feature of the principles forming the basis of the demand is what Boumedienne had dwelt upon: *the economic sovereignty of nations*, which means complete national control over natural resources and overall economic activities, including the right to nationalization. The demands cover specific areas principally dealing with international trade, aid, foreign investment, transfer of technology, and the international monetary system. But the centerpiece of these specific demands is the issue of trade, which calls for international agreements on commodities aimed at raising and stabilizing the price of raw materials, and an increase in the volume of exports from the Third World to the industrialized countries with reduced tariffs.

In December 1974, the UN General Assembly adopted a Charter of Economic Rights and Duties of States to promote the principles of a new international economic order. The right to nationalization is recognized under the charter, "with appropriate compensation" to be made according to the laws of the nationalizing state. In case of dispute over compensation, "it shall be settled under the domestic law of the nationalizing State and by its tribunal,"[20] unless otherwise agreed mutually.

The use of oil and the threat of similar use of other primary commodities—which was previously a source of mild amusement for the powerful—now produced some dramatic results. The significance of the declaration of the Charter of Economic Rights and Duties lies in the legitimation of the demands of the Third World by the international community represented at the United Nations. The consequences of "legitimation" of the Third World demands has been to move from confrontation to "dialogue." The focus shifted from New York to Paris and the form became the Conference on International Economic Cooperation or the Paris "North-South Dialogue," as it has been called. The Paris "Dialogue" ended in a deadlock, after 18 months of negotiations marked by bitter wrangling.

The final joint communique which came at the end of the meetings noted that progress had been made but registered "regrets" by both sides that they had not bridged their differences. From the "Northerners" point of view, the most significant failure was their inability to deal with OPEC separately to secure an agreement on energy supplies and pricing, which was the main reason for their participation. From the "Southerners" point of view, a comprehensive agreement on trade and aid in accordance with the principles of the demands for a new international economic orders was sought but rejected.

The major obstacle of the Third World as a "trade union of nations" is still the weakness of their bargaining position. Where the demanding side cannot "induce fear in the opponent," progress comes very slowly, if at all as Branislav Gosovic aptly put it.[21] And so the silent battle continues, as it does between labor and capital within the national boundaries of all capitalist countries. The poor buy or sell at whatever price suits the wealthy.[22] It is clear that economic self-determination, no less than its political counterpart, needs organized force behind it in order to make significant gains. The "poor" nations must create and maintain a system of organized collective self-reliance.

NOTES

1. *The Lansing Papers* 1914-1920, US Department of State, 1939. See also, Robert Lansing, *The Peace Negotiations* (London: Houghton, Mifflin Company, Boston and New York, 1921), p. 87.
2. Preface to the Polish Edition (1892) of the Communist *Manifesto.*
3. Joan Robinson, *Economic Philosophy*, Pelican Books, 1964, p. 10.
4. *Ibid.*
5. Stewart Chase, *How Language Shapes Our Thoughts*, 1954, p. 100.
6. Rupert Emerson, *Empire to Nation*, Cambridge: Harvard University Press, 1960, p. 197.
7. *Ibid.*
8. Thomas Hodgkin, *Nationalism in Colonial Africa*, Pelican Books, 1956, p. 17.
9. Emerson, *op cit.*, p. 24-25.
10. Sallie T. Selle (ed), *The Rediscovery of Ethnicity*, 1974.
11. Wilton S. Dillon, E. Plurubus Unum, *The Cultural Drama*, Washington: Smithsonian Institution, 1974, p. 39-40.
12. Lord Hailey, *An African Survey*, Oxford: Oxford University Press, 193.
13. "African Socialism Revisited," *African Forum*, I.3(1966):6.
14. *Op cit.*, p. 306.
15. *Ibid.*, p. 307-308.
16. See Richard Barnet and Muller, *Global Reach, The Power of Multi-National Corporations.* See also C. Arrighi and J. Saul, "Essays on the Political Economy of Africa," *Monthly Review*, 1973, pp. 105-143.

17. The Dependence Theorists are typified by Raul Prebisch, Andre Guntar Frank, and Samir Amin.
18. See also, *Non-Aligment in an Age of Alignments*, A.W. Singham and Shirley Hune, Zed Press, 1986.
19. P. Tullock, *The Politics of Preferences*, London, 1975.
20. UN Public Information, UN Today, "Suggestions for Speakers," New York: UN Publications, 1977, p. 52.
21. UNCTAD, *Conflict and Compromise*, 1971.
22. Julius K. Nyerere, "The Economic Challenge. Dialogue or Confrontation," an address to the Royal Commonwealth Society, London, 1975.

Chapter 4
The Law of Self-Determination and the Eritrean Case

INTRODUCTION

The principle of self-determination has been one of the salient features of the law of nations since the post-World War II era. It holds that all people have the right to shape their destiny and, notably in the case of dependent peoples, to determine their political future. The mechanisms by which such rights are determined is also today subject to general agreement, and is an important feature of contemporary international law. By whatever name it is known—referendum, plebiscite, etc.—such a mechanism necessarily involves the *direct* participation of any dependent people in determining their political future, under the auspices of an impartial body, normally the United Nations and/or a regional organization. Any departure from such procedure would be unacceptable today as an infringement of an established, fundamental principle of law.

Self-determination is a concept which began as a moral precept expressing humanity's outrage against all forms of subjugation and bondage. Its development in the "adventure of ideas," therefore, represents a highwater-mark in moral evolution. It first gained political currency with the enthronement of reason as a guide to political and social action during the 17th and 18th centuries in Europe, and then again at the conclusion of World War I.

It was finally elevated to the status of a universally applicable normative order after World War II, with the creation of the United Nations and the decline of the imperial idea and the European colonial empires built upon that idea. The charter of the United Nations and the Universal Declaration of Human Rights of 1948 provided the legal anchor to a hitherto authoritative but, controversial, political and moral concept.[1]

This codification of a key political/moral concept, like all codifications, mainly reflects man's emphatic commitment to the idea. Codifications remove the shadows of doubt and controversy that may surround any concept. At the same time, self-determination is not just any codified legal principle, but a higher principle which is itself the source of other legal principles that are the subject matter of national constitutions and other "municipal laws." In that sense, therefore, it is an epochal principle and a measure of the evolution of the international community—a significant milestone in man's long and slippery spiritual ascent. The complexity and hazards of this journey need not be demonstrated in any detail, beyond pointing to the history of slavery, colonial rule, the holocaust, and Stalin's purges, not to mention the unmentionable—the fate of the "American Indians." That a good deal of emotion is invested in the invocation of self-determination by concerned groups should not be a source of wonder in the light of history and the continuation of oppression in many corners of the world. At the same time the establishment of the concept as a universal law means that we do not need to argue against the evils of apartheid, which are evident and universally condemned. Apartheid cannot be reformed; it has to be swept away.[2]

The majority of the members of the United Nations were emancipated from colonial rule through different forms of struggle, or passed through different timetables of decolonization. In each case self-determination was the central principle invoked to achieve decolonization. What then can we make of those cases where this principle was not applied, where politics was allowed to prevail over legal principle and the right of peoples to determine their futures? The United Nations 1950 Resolution on Eritrea, which substituted the decision of that organization for the right of the Eritrean people to determine their future, remains an unresolved paradox in the annals of international law, as will be explained in this essay.

As previously noted, modern history of the "disposal" of the Eritrean question begins after the end of World War II. Following the defeat of Italy, Eritrea's colonizer, and the failure of the four victorious powers (USA, USSR, Britain, and France) to agree on the disposal of Italy's fomer colonies (Eritrea, Libya, and Somalia), the matter was submitted to the General Assembly of the United Nations, in accordance with the Pact of Paris.

Under that treaty, Italy renounced her claims to her former colonies and the Four Powers agreed to submit the case to the UN General Assembly, in the event of disagreement.

The UN General Assembly decided the future of Libya and Somalia with comparative ease, but failed to agree on Eritrea. After three years of protracted debate and a report from the Commission of Enquiry, the fate of Eritrea was decided, conforming to the compromise favored by the United States of America. American strategic and geopolitical interests converged with the ambitions of Emperor Haile Selassie of Ethiopia. Resolution 390 A(v) of 1950 was passed, federating Eritrea as an "autonomous unit under the sovereignty of the Ethiopian Crown." This resolution failed to meet the demands of the majority of the Eritrean people; they wanted independence.

A point of interest implicit in the Eritrean story concerns the relation (and the gap) between law and politics. It is pertinent that law and politics are different, but related social phenomena. Although in a general sense law is part of politics in terms of its social origin and dynamics, the boundary between law and politics is distinct in a fundamental sense and must be clearly drawn. Discussion of this point in any detail is beyond the scope of the present essay. Jurists of different times and climes have grappled with the concept of law and what differentiates it from orders backed by force, from morality, etc. Politics in its mundane application may be simply stated as who gets what, when, and how; and law may be used as the instrument for the resolution of these questions. It is nonetheless distinct from politics both in theory and practice.

In what follows, we will consider the law of self-determination in contemporary international law in general, and its application to the Eritrean case in particular.

THE LAW OF SELF-DETERMINATION

As already noted, self-determination is an established principle of international law. As such, it is not subject to debate or disagreement between East and West or "North" and "South," although differences may occur sometimes on the manner or timing of its application. The Eritrean case is unique from the standpoint of modern international law in that the principle was not applied at all to this former colonial territory which qualifies for its application in every respect as will be explained.

The principal code which has been the source of international law in the post-World War II era is the charter of the United Nations. The articles relevant to this discussion provide that primary among the purposes of the United Nations is:

> to provide friendly relations among nations based on respect for the principle of equal rights and self-determination of peoples, and to take appropriate measures to strengthen universal peace...³

and

> to be a centre for harmonizing the actions of nations in the attainment of these common ends.⁴.

Another provision of the charter stipulates that

> with a view to the creation of conditions of stability and well-being which are necessary for peaceful and friendly relations among nations based on respect for the principle of equal rights and self-determination of peoples, the United Nations shall promote: higher standards of living... etc.⁵

Another basic instrument of international law is the Universal Declaration of Human Rights of 1948, which was proclaimed "as a common standard of achievement for all peoples and nations..." Its preamble is an eloquent reminder that "recognition of the inherent dignity and of the equal and inalienable rights of all members of the human family is the foundation of freedom, justice and peace in the world" and that "disregard and contempt for human rights have resulted in barbarous acts which have outraged the conscience of mankind..." Human rights should be protected by the rule of law, "if man is not to be compelled to have recourse, as a last resort, to rebellion against tyranny and oppression."

There is an interesting point of history, not without irony, in the fact that the USSR abstained in the final vote when the declaration was adopted. The reason is partly ideological and partly a reflection of the East-West tension at the time, developing from the Berlin crisis. Ideologically, socialist jurisprudence lays stress on the importance of peoples' rights in contrast to Western (Lockean) emphasis on individual human rights. On the other hand, Soviet literature expresses the importance of *national* rights to self-determination, in principle. Indeed some Soviet writers assert, with good reason, that the October Socialist Revolution of 1917 quickened the pace of decolonization.⁶

Starushenko writes "Soviet Russia not only proclaimed new principles in international relations but added a democratic, anticolonial content to a number of old principles."⁷ But in the same breath, he says:

> The principle of self determination is a new international rule, for unlike its predecessor, the bourgeois principle of nationality, it does

not necessarily stipulate secession but implies the possibility of various nations and nationalities into a big state on a federal or other basis.[8]

The grain of dialectical contradiction and its implications is a story that must be left to another day. Here it is enough to say that it provides flexibility to Soviet foreign and domestic (constitutional) policy concerning the rights of nations. It is a sobering fact of history that the Soviet position on the Eritrean question in 1950 was the same as that of Czechoslovakia (quoted above), and that today the Soviet Union supports the reverse, now opposing Eritrean national self-determination.

On the other hand, it is undeniable that the Soviet Union helped to initiate the resolution on decolonization which further elucidates the principle of self-determination. Adopted on December 14, 1960 and subtitled "A Resolution on the Granting of Independence to Colonial Countries and Peoples," that landmark resolution amplified Articles 1 and 55 of the UN Charter and the Universal Declaration of Human Rights. It declared that "all peoples have the right to self-determination" and that by virtue of that right they determine their political status and freely pursue their economic, social and cultural development."[9] The Resolution also declares that "the subjection of peoples to alien subjugation and exploitation... is contrary to the Charter of the United Nations..." Then, on November 4, 1970, the General Assembly passed Resolution 2625(xxv) concerning the principles of international law governing "Friendly Relations and Co-operation Among States."

These two Resolutions reinforce the right of peoples to free themselves from foreign rule and also introduced a new element, that is, the right of peoples to be complete masters of their own affairs in an independent state. Another resolution of the UN General Assembly reaffirmed "the right of peoples under colonial rule to exercise their rights of self-determination and independence" and "the right of every nation, large or small, to choose freely and without any external interference its political, social and economic system."[10]

The charter of the Organization of African Unity (OAU) adopted in 1963 also provides a regional underpinning to the law of nations. The charter reaffirms the principle of self-determination of peoples,[11] the sovereign equality among nations, noninterference in internal affairs, territorial integrity, peaceful settlement of disputes, and non-alignment.[12] The OAU also reaffirmed the colonially fixed boundaries to define African postcolonial statehood.[13]

The effect of the end of colonial rule is to convert people from being *objects* of alien rule to being *subjects* of rights and obligations. But it is one thing to be subject of rights and obligations, and quite another to exercise those rights freely and to an optimal degree. This requires favorable international as well as domestic conditions which may be absent due to external interference or domestic turmoil.

The international legal strategy to achieve such conditions was devised under two international covenants on human rights which expanded the frontiers of self-determination, pushing it further from where it was left under the important resolutions mentioned before. These covenants, adopted by the UN General Assembly and offered for ratification to member states in 1966, came into force ten years later, in 1976.[15]

The covenants stipulated that "all *peoples* have rights to self-determination." But even before their ratification, the covenants had already attained authoritative recognition. This was illustrated by the opinion of the International Court of Justice (ICJ) concerning Namibia (South West Africa).[16] The ICJ's opinion was also given in the case of Western Sahara.[17] In both instances, the Court took note of the "validity" of the principle of self-determination" as "a right of peoples."[18]

The absence of conditions favorable to the exercise of self-determination in all its dimensions, as stipulated by the covenants, may also be and often is caused by internal problems. The agony of many nations in the world today, though in many instances aggravated by external intervention, is rooted in histories of domestic conflict, and the failure of the states to provide a framework for just and equitable accommodations to demands of social or political groups within their borders. The Horn of Africa is a prime example in which two factors combine to perpetuate a cycle of conflict and devastation. The Eritrean case falls in a special category among the various conflicts of the region, in view of its colonial history and unconsummated decolonization.

ERITREA AND INTERNATIONAL LAW

Eritrea as a territorial entity is a creation of colonial history, like most other countries of Africa. When Italian colonial rule came to an end with Italy's defeat in 1941, the victorious British forces replaced Italian colonial rule and administered Eritrea for over ten years until the United Nations Resolution came into force in September 1952. Emperor Haile Selassie's government succeeded the British administration.

Legally, Italian colonial rule came to an end with the signing of the Pact of Paris in 1946, when Italy formally renounced her claims over her former colonies. Eritrea became a ward of Great Britain, pending its disposal by the General Assembly of the United Nations to which the Allied Powers had submitted the case for determination. The reasons for the failure of the United Nations to apply the full measure of self-determination with respect to the Eritrean people, by arranging a referendum, preferring to impose a federal arrangement with Ethiopia, and the consequences of that failure are documented elsewhere.[19]

John Foster Dulles bluntly expressed the stakes which caused the denial of the principle of self-determination.* Documents have come to light, thanks to the US Freedom of Information Act, adding more details on the strategic rationale and the diplomatic maneouvers that went into this denial.[20] Leaving the history of diplomatic maneouvers, we need to focus on the legal consequences of that history. Following Italian and British colonial rule, the next legal "source" of the status of Eritrea was the resolution of the UN General Assembly which federated it with Ethiopia.[21] The resolution provided for an autonomous Eritrean government with legislative, executive, and judicial powers over domestic affairs; matters of defense, foreign affairs, currency and finance, foreign and "interstate" trade, and communication would fall under "federal" (Ethiopian) jurisdiction.

The "federal" arrangement lacked an essential element of the federal principle, that is, equality between the component entities with an impartial arbiter to settle any conflicts or disputes that might arise between (or among) the entities. Eritrea was an unequal partner in the federal arrangement. The head of the federation was the Ethiopian emperor whose foreign minister vehemently had opposed at the United Nations any arrangement short of complete union.[22]

Subsequent events and new information indicate beyond doubt that the unequal status of Eritrea, and the lack of an impartial arbiter, was known to the major actors who shaped Eritrea's destiny.[23]

Nor was there provision made in the arrangement for a neutral institution and for procedures to mediate conflicts or settle disputes between the entities. It was obviously in recognition of this glaring gap that Anze Matienzo, the UN Commissioner on Eritrea who oversaw the transition, observed in his final report that Resolution 390 A(v) would remain an international instrument and that the UN General Assembly would be seized of the matter, in the event of any violation of its provisions.

The worst fears of those who opposed the federal arrangement were confirmed when Emperor Haile Selassie abrogated the UN resolution,

---

*"From the point of view of justice the opinion of the Eritrean people must receive consideration. Nevertheless, the strategic interests of the United States in the Red Sea Basin and world peace make it necessary that the country be linked with our ally Ethiopia."

abolishing the federation and declaring Eritrea a province of Ethiopia.[24] This outcome confirmed the view that the resolution was an instrument for gradual incorporation of Eritrea into the Ethiopian Empire.

THE LEGAL EFFECT OF RESOLUTION 390 A(V)

We noted the gap between the requirements of international law declared in the UN Charter and the Universal Declaration of Human Rights, and the UN General Assembly's application (or non-application) in the Eritrean case. What then is the effect of Resolution 390 A(v)? What rights and obligations did the resolution confer and on whom? And can a grant of autonomy to Eritrea, short of complete independence, constitute the application of the right to self-determination; or does it constitute, as indicated before, a denial of that right?

Clearly, the resolution was not an instrument of what may now be called classical decolonization under which a colonial ruler transfers, or is induced to transfer, power completely to the colonized peoples. Its principal sponsors, and those who joined them in the majority vote to secure its passage, were either not supporters of the idea that colonial rule was rendered illegal by the Charter, or if they were, other considerations weighed more heavily. Their dilemmas and designs are revealed in the preamble to the resolution. It offers a clue to providing an answer to the legal questions being probed here. The preamble reads, in part:

> Taking into consideration: (a) the wishes and welfare of the inhabitants of Eritrea, including the views of the various racial and political groups of the provinces of the territory and the capacity of the people for self-government; (b) the interests of peace and security in East Africa; (c) the rights and claims of Ethiopia on geographical, historical, ethnic or economic reason, including in particular Ethiopia's legitimate need for adequate access to the sea...

Apart from the fact that peace was made conditional upon the sacrifice of self-determination in satisfying Ethiopian demands (and the interests of its supporters at the time), the preamble reveals the inability of that United Nations General Assembly to reject the colonial ideology of viewing people in fractured terms (ethnic, racial, etc.) and of insisting on their "capacity for self-government" and economic viability. By stipulating "the capacity of the people for self-government," the resolution accommodates the earlier colonial view of controlled change by stages.[25] Resolution 1514 put an end to such stipulation; the inadequacy of political, economic, social, or educational preparedness was henceforth rejected as a pretext for delaying decolonization.

In sum, the obvious and primary effect of Resolution 390 was to deny Eritreans the exercise of their right to full self-determination. Second, it defined the legal status of the territorial entity called Eritrea as distinct from Ethiopia. Third, it defined the status of the inhabitants of this territory as a *people* within the meaning of international law. It did all this as the basic source of the Federal Act and the Eritrean Constitution, which incorporated its essential elements.

(a) Denial of self-determination: This has already been touched upon. Here we need only reiterate the inherent contradiction between this denial and the UN Charter, and also point out the contradiction between this denial and the recognition of Eritrean territory and the Eritrean people as distinct from those of Ethiopia. Such denial, dictated by the logic of strategic arguments, assumed legal significance when later the terms of the resolution were violated *in toto.*

(b) Territory: The Ethiopian claim that Eritrea was historically part of Ethiopia and that colonial history did not, or could not, change the claim for "recovery" was not accepted by the United Nations. The words of the preamble quoted above, and others throughout the text of the resolution and the derivative laws of Eritrea, recognized it as a distinct territorial entity.[26] Parts of southern Eritrea and parts of northern Ethiopia did once form part of the Axumite Empire, which broke up long before Columbus discovered America.[27] The critical period of history which defined the broad outlines of African development including that of Eritrea (including the fixing of boundaries), is European colonial history. In Eritrea's case, the Ethiopian Emperor Menelik II recognized this by signing a treaty with Italy.[28]

(c) People: The expression "people" is used by the resolution three times: (i) in the preamble (the capacity of the people . . .); (ii) in reference to convening a representative assembly of Eritreans "chosen by the people" (paragraph 11); and (iii) in paragraph 12, stating that the constitution of Eritrea "shall contain provisions adopting and ratifying the Federal Act on behalf of the people of Eritrea."

The use of the word was not accidental, needless to say. It plainly was the outcome of a conscious choice made by the General Assembly, particularly in view of Ethiopia's contention during the debates preceding the adoption of the Resolution, that Ethiopians and Eritreans are one people.[29] One misfortune of the Eritrean people was their "choice" of the wrong colonizer! Had their original European colonizer been either British or

French, their right to exercise self-determination would not have come prematurely, before the adoption of Resolution 1514 (xv). Then the logic of being recognized as a people would have impelled the UN General Assembly to allow them to exercise that right to the fullest extent. For example, Djibouti, a former French colony, was granted independence, with a population of 300,000 (one tenth of Eritrea) and with a resource-poor territory (21,800 Sq. Kms. compared to Eritrea's 120,000 Sq. Kms. and much better resource endowment).

The Permanent Peoples Tribunal recognized the Eritreans as a people under international law. In its final opinion, the Tribunal declared:

> The Eritrean people did not constitute a national minority within a state. They have the characteristics of a people according to the law of the United Nations and the Universal Declaration of the Rights of People.

and

> the identity of the Eritrean people determined, in particular, by its resistance to Italian colonialism was recognized by Resolution 390 A(v) of the General Assembly of the United Nations.[30]

The International Commission of Jurists has summed up this question, thus: "... the Eritreans have as much right to be considered as a "people" as the people of most African countries which were created by the division of Africa among the imperial powers at the end of the 19th century."[31] The Commission might have added that, in tandem with the European imperial process, an Ethiopian imperial process of conquest and expansion was taking place to the south, southwest and southeast of Emperor Menelik's central kingdom. This expansion brought under its control over seventy different nationalities and over two-thirds of today's Ethiopia.[32]

From the foregoing it is clear that the expectations of Eritreans for complete independence were well-founded. Resolution 390 A(v), though recognizing them and their country as distinct, fell short of enabling them to fulfill those expectations in a full acquisition of sovereign nationhood. The abolition of the less than perfect federation at the very moment when other African peoples were attaining such sovereign nationhood could only add to their resolve to reclaim their right—hence, the explosion of the armed struggle to be considered below; hence also their persistence against incredible odds, particularly since the Soviet switch to support Ethiopia.

THE LEGAL EFFECT OF THE ABOLITION OF THE FEDERATION: PREVAILING CONDITIONS AND PROCEDURES

It should be pointed out that the emperor of Ethiopia, through his representative, did everything in his power to subvert the integrity of the federation or Eritrean autonomy. His representative, who under the Federal Act, was to exercise ceremonial functions only, did in fact go beyond ceremony. He actively sought to foster division within the Eritrean government, and as early as 1953 struck down one of the pillars of the system: freedom of the press.*

On order of the Ethiopian representative, a legal suit was brought against the *Voice of Eritrea*. The "federal high court," whose judges were appointed at the emperor's pleasure, suspended the publication of that newspaper and sentenced its editors to six years imprisonment. The government imposed a ban on newspapers not sponsored or controlled by it. The Eritrean political parties sent a cable to the United Nations on October 12, 1953 protesting this violation. There was no UN response.[33] This was prelude to more violations which the Eritrean Assembly protested in a resolution it passed on May 22, 1954, pressing the Eritrean Chief Executive to seek UN intervention in the event of the emperor's failure to call a halt to these violations. The Assembly repeated its demands so vehemently and repeatedly that the emperor's representative convened a meeting in which he went to issue a severe reprimand including, notably, the following injunction:

> There are no internal or external affairs as far as the office of his Imperial Majesty's representative is concerned, and there will be none in the future. The affairs of Eritrea concern Ethiopia as a whole and the Emperor.

Five months later, the Eritrean chief executive, who was elected by the Eritrean assembly under the constitution, was removed under imperial pressure, and appointed as Ethiopia's ambassador to Sweden. He was replaced by a handpicked chief executive, who was later to read the resolution dissolving the federation. The protest movement of the Eritrean people, which took different forms, at different levels of intensity, orig-

---

*This information and much of that in the following paragraphs was obtained through interviews of living witnesses including some living in Eritrea now, whose identity cannot be revealed.

inated in these violations of the terms of the federation. There were petitions, student protests, demonstrations, and finally, in 1958 following the banning of the labor unions, a nationwide strike lasting several days. in 1957, the emperor's government replaced the Eritrean languages by Amharic as language of instruction and communication. It removed the Eritrean flag in November 1959; the seal of the Eritrean government was withdrawn in June 1960. The Eritrean liberation movement was organized clandestinely, as arrests and preventive detention measures were routinely applied. Finally, in September 1961, the peaceful phase of the protest movement gave way to the armed phase of the Eritrean national liberation with the establishment of the Eritrean Liberation Front (ELF).

Abolition of the federation was announced to the world on November 15, 1962. The instrument for carrying out the abolition was (Imperial) Order No. 27, 1962. It should be pointed out that Order No. 27 had been prepared in Addis Ababa long before the gist of it was read to the Eritrean assembly on November 15, 1962. The circumstances surrounding that event are so extraordinary that a summary of some crucial events on the eve of the abolition is in order to underline this travesty of the legislative/constitutional process.

> *November 5, 1962*—the Eritrean Chief Executive left for Addis Ababa and returned in the company of the Prime Minister on November 7. The latter stayed in Asmara until November 10 holding briefs and intense consultations.
>
> *November 10-13, 1962*—Eritrean members of the Assembly were summoned to the Assembly to be given lectures on the need to abolish the federation by the Vice President of the Assembly, an Ethiopian Orthodox cleric, known for his unionist leanings. In an atmosphere of siege, with the Assembly surrounded by armed police, the members were told to vote dissolving the federation. They refused. There was an uproar, and some members were roughed up.
>
> *November 13, 1962*—the Chief Executive, who had flown to Addis Ababa on November 11 to meet the Emperor and his Prime Minister, returned to Asmara. He ordered the police contingent on duty surrounding the Assembly building to relinquish its duties. Ethiopian troops staged a demonstration in the city, with the air force flying low, and intimidating slogans were shouted. "To him who refuses give him a bullet."[34] Then a detachment of the armed forces took position around the Assembly building.

November 14, 1962—Eritrean deputies were once again summoned; those who protested were brought by force, and some were beaten up. The Vice President assumed his chair at 10:35 a.m. and called the meeting to order, announcing that the Chief Executive would come to the Assembly to table an important motion. The Chief Executive entered the Assembly building at 10:45 a.m., accompanied by the Secretaries of his government. He delivered a speech and tabled a motion. The words of the preamble of his motion ("whereas we are aware that the name 'federation' finds no place in our history or our tradition..," etc.) are similar to the preamble of Order No. 27 which entered into force the same day.

Order No. 27 declared:

> The federal status of Eritrea and Ethiopia is hereby terminated and Eritrea, which continues to constitute an integral part of Ethiopia is hereby wholly integrated into the unitary system of administration of our Empire.[35]

It then extended the constitution of Ethiopia to Eritrea.

The Czechoslovakian delegate's prophetic predictrion (quoted above) came to pass. Sir Ivor Jennings, the eminent British constitutional authority who was one of the panel of jurists who drafted the Eritrean constitution, had expressed the dilemma facing his panel. The dilemma was how to work out a constitution "for a democratic state federated with Ethiopia" which, by implication, meant a nondemocratic Ethiopia.[36]

Politically, the effect of the annexation was to galvanize Eritrean resistance. For, whatever its limitation, the federal arrangement gave the Eritreans some room to maneouver which they now completely lost. The timing was also clever, from the emperor's point of view. It occurred six months before the first meeting of the OAU (the founding conference) was due to be held in Addis Ababa, with the emperor as host. His aim was to present Africa the *fait accompli* of an annexed Eritrea with its colonial boundaries obliterated. Though unsuccessful, Eritreans made attempts to petition the African heads of state and government.

Legally, the effect of Order No. 27 was first of all to remove all the rights and privileges which Eritreans were guaranteed under the Federal Act and the Eritrean constitution derived from the UN resolution. At this point it will be helpful to recapitulate the main features of the resolution which guaranteed those rights.

- It implicitly recognized the national identity of the Eritrean people and the territorial unity of Eritrea pursuant to the colonially fixed boundaries.
- It provided for an autonomous Eritrean government with clearly defined domestic jurisdiction in legislative, executive, and judicial matters.
- It guaranteed the Eritrean people "the fullest respect and safeguards for their institutions, traditions, religions, and languages . . . "
- It guaranteed all persons in Eritrea the enjoyment of human rights and fundamental freedoms through provision of a Bill of Rights and Fundamental Freedoms.
- It enshrined the democratic principle in Article 16 of the Eritrean Constitution, which was the foundation of the above-listed rights and fundamental freedoms. Moreover, Article 16 was not to be amended under any circumstances.

The second legal effect of the abolition was to reaffirm the Eritrean peoples' right to full self-determination. The dissolution of the federation was the climax of a process which originated at the United Nations with denial of full self-determination. To use a metaphor, the chains forged to fetter the full measure of independence—albeit rather lengthened chains—were broken by the act of dissolution, releasing the Eritreans once more to wage a national liberation struggle. As the Permanent Peoples Tribunal has observed,

> Today, it is not a question of judging the legitimacy of the "secession" of Eritrea from Ethiopia. It is, on the contrary, a question of taking note of the failure of a resolution proposed by the General Assembly of the United Nations in 1950, and therefore re-examining the problem of the self-determination of the Eritrean people.[37]

And as the International Commission of Jurists has argued, assuming that the Eritrean people were presumed to have accepted the resolution, the people have the right to claim independence afresh "if the federal state concerned denies its democratic rights to the people who have opted to join it."[38]

The opposing view on the Ethiopian side turns on the principle of respect for territorial integrity of a state. Both the United Nations and the OAU uphold that as a primary norm in international law. The most explicit authority for that norm is Resolution 2526 (xxv) of 1970 which stipulates that exercise of the right of peoples to self-determination cannot take precedence over the principle of respect for the territorial integrity of states. The OAU Charter also subscribes to this principle.

Now, the OAU was established in 1963. But it does not mean that the OAU was then, or is now, committed to guaranteeing unity between Ethiopia and Eritrea. To do so would be tantamount to undermining the foundation of the post-colonial African legal order. One of the cardinal points of that order is that the state system was defined by the colonially fixed boundaries. As the Peoples Tribunal has opined:

> The OAU could, at its creation, only take note of the existing *de jure* and *de facto* situation. Ethiopia in 1963 and thereafter, had, and has done nothing more than occupy de facto a territory which it had promised the United Nations to administer in accordance with a federal system.[39]

This situation, illegal under the terms of the United Nations doctrine, could not in 1963, and cannot now, be legitimized under the doctrine of the OAU, which is a regional organization required to act in accordance with the aims and principles of the United Nations.[40]

The UN General Assembly itself has provided a built-in principle—a criterion—for mediating between the two primary norms in the event of conflict. Resolution 2526 (xxv) states:

> Nothing in the foregoing paragraphs shall be construed as authorizing or encouraging any action which would dismember or impair, totally or in part, the territorial integrity or political unity of sovereign and independent states, *conducting themselves in compliance with the principle of equal rights and self-determination of peoples as described above and thus possessed of a government representing the whole people belonging to the territory without distinction as to race, creed or colour.* (Italics added)

It is difficult to overstress the importance attached to respect for territorial integrity, particularly in the African context. The history of the Katanga (Shaba) rebellion and of the Biafra attempts at secession, and the depth of passion with which these attempts were fought attests to the importance of the principle. On the whole, it is remarkable that few such attempts have been made, given the ethnic diversity within the post-colonial nation-states of Africa. Colonial history, it seems, has forged a higher kind of allegiance defined by a common history of struggle and a sense of nationhood within the confines of artificially drawn boundaries, cross-cutting ethnic lines.

In this respect, the case of Cameroun is instructive. Camouroun was divided between the British and the French after it was taken from the Germans, following the latter's World War I defeat in 1918. The British ruled their part of Cameroun for some forty years, whereas German rule over the whole of Cameroun lasted some thirty years. Yet the people of the northern part of British Cameroun, on a referendum, chose to join the rest of Cameroun and not the English-speaking Nigeria. In other words, German rule became the colonial "patrimony" by reference to which a people decided their political future.

This point underscores the importance of colonial history. It does not mean that Africans are celebrating colonial rule. It means they accepted a fact of history—an accomplished fact—and used it as a basis to build a new political future. The case of Eritrea is no exception.

The commitment of the OAU, no less than the United Nations, to the principle of respect for territorial integrity is demonstrable. But in the case of Eritrea one cannot speak of the infringement of territorial integrity of Ethiopia. As we have seen, the territorial distinctiveness of the two has been recognized by the United Nations. The federal solution of 1950 was only a compromise imposed as a partial fulfillment of self-determination for the Eritrean people. The failure of that, caused by Ethiopia's violation of the UN resolution, cannot negate the distinctiveness of Eritrea as a territory, or deny the Eritrean people their right to self-determination.

In terms of UN Resolution 2526 (xxv), the above-quoted crucial passage provides the key to resolving the conflicts between the two international norms. It defines the relationship between equal rights and self-determination on the one hand, and the respect for the territorial integrity of states on the other, by making the latter principle conditional upon the observance of the former. Where there is a clear violation of the principle of equal rights and self-determination, this right would prevail over that of territorial integrity.

In the Eritrean case, specific historical circumstances creating specific legal situations call for comments in addition to the above. The emperor of Ethiopia and the members of the Eritrean Assembly—even assuming that that no duress was applied, which clearly was—were under the obligation to uphold and preserve the federation and the laws under it. The Eritrean deputies were sworn to defend the Eritrean constitution and the rights of the Eritrean people under it, and had not mandate to assent to the overthrow of the system without a referendum, or other form of popular participation. The Eritrean constitution provides that the assembly "may not, by means of an amendment, introduce into the constitution any provision which would not be in conformity with the Federal Act."[41] And there was a prohibition to amend Article 16 of the constitution "by the terms of which the constitution of Eritrea was based on the principle of democratic government."[42]

Applying the terms of Resolution 2526 (xxv), it is clear that abolition of the federation and incorporation of Eritrea as an Ethiopian province was not "in compliance with the principle of equal rights and self-determination." In the words of the International Commission of Jurists:

> Since the people of Eritrea, *ex hypothesi*, agreed to union with Ethiopia only as an autonomous unit, the abolition of the status and its integration within Ethiopia cannot be regarded as being in compliance with equal rights and self-determination of peoples unless there was a clear and unequivocal decision by the people of Eritrea in favor of that change.[43]

CONCLUSION: ERITREA IS UNIQUELY A UN RESPONSIBILITY

With the failure of international legal and moral principles to mediate between conflicting forces, war has been the final arbiter. This has invited the involvement of foreign powers and has thus meant the internationalization of the conflict. As the scale of the war, and the involvement of foreign powers, increased with the consequence of more casualties and devastation of the civilian population, the need for involvement by the United Nations becomes more urgent.

With the advent of a radical military regime in Ethiopia and the involvement of the Soviet Union on the Ethiopian side, the scale of the war has increased tenfold, from 12,000 to over 120,000 Ethiopian troops involved in Eritrea alone. Eight major offensives have been launched against the Eritrean national liberation fighters since 1978, all advised by Soviet officers, using Soviet-supplied military hardware, including sophisticated artillery, armory, fighterjets, and bombers.[44]

In this incredible drama, it is remarkable that it is the side with the greater firepower, which is also a sovereign state, that has called for the intervention of a great power in its war against its smaller adversary. There is no foreign power involved on Eritrea's side, militarily or otherwise. The secret of the survival of the Eritrean war of liberation in the face of such heavy odds lies in the fact that it is what Karl Deutch calls "an authentic war or revolution."[45] The absence of foreign military aid and the overall self-reliance of the Eritreans qualifies the war as such. But the historical and legal analyses attempted in this essay place the Eritrean case on a higher plane, beyond an academic, analytical category. The Eritrean case calls for unequivocal declaration by the organized bodies of the international community, especially the United Nations and the OAU, that it is just.

As to the question of whether the United Nations is entitled to intervene today, the weight of authoritative juristic answer is categorically in the affirmative. The UN General Assembly's responsibility did not end with the adoption of Resolution 390 A(v) or its coming into force in 1952. As Anze Mateinzo, the UN Commissioner of Eritrea, and his panel of jurists put it:

With regard to the application of the General Assembly's Resolution after the entry into force of the Federal Act and the Eritrean Constitution have come into force the mission entrusted the General Assembly under the Peace Treaty with Italy will have been fulfilled and that the future of Eritrea must be regarded as settled, but it does not follow that the United Nations would no longer have any right to deal with the question. The United Nations Resolution of Eritrea would remain an international instrument and, if violated, the General Assembly could be seized of the matter.[46]

The United Nations is thus not only entitled but duty-bound to intervene in the Eritrean case. The Ethiopian government knows that it cannot avail itself of the UN Charter's provision prohibiting UN intervention in the domestic affairs of the state.[47] That prohibition must be read together with Resolution 390 A(v) and other relevant resolutions of the United Nations, as discussed above. It may reasonably be presumed that it was such realization, and an awareness of the legal force behind the Eritrean cause, which prompted the Ethiopian authorities to issue a secret memorandum instructing their diplomats to stay clear of any involvement in legal arguments over the issue; but also to stress, instead, politico-stratgic imperatives.[48]

The Permanent People's Tribunal draws a parallel between the Eritrean case and those of Namibia and Western Sahara. In both those cases, the International Court of Justice has given authoritative opinion in favor of the self-determination for the peoples of Namibia and Western Sahara. And, in its verdict, the Permanent People's Tribunal states that the Eritrean question lies within the competence of the United Nations on two counts: "the maintenance of international peace and security and the obligation to guarantee respect for the right of peoples to self-determination."[49]

The centrality of the principle of self-determination in international law today has been unequivocally affirmed by the International Court of Justice, which is traditionally cautious. The People's Tribunal has echoed that opinion with equal emphasis in a number of cases. And, as Friedman has written, in the development of general principles of law, "more important judicial advance will continue to come from special international tribunals, or from arbitration tribunals . . . "[50]

What then are the reasons why the United Nations has failed to take the Eritrean case which clearly falls within its competence? The reasons are political, not legal. Geography and history, it seems, conspired against the Eritrean people to cause their denial of independence or, as the People's Tribunal put it, to set them on a course of "false decolonization."[51] Of all the formerly colonized peoples in the world, the Eritreans suffered the worst fate due to the strategic and geopolitical rivalries of powers greater than them. The strategic location of their country and the territorial ambition of a famous emperor, which coincided with the interests of the United States, sealed their fate, denying them the fruits of decolonization which had been universally declared as being due all colonized peoples.

Today, that same strategic location has turned the Soviet Union against them after an earlier support of their case for independence. Paradoxically, Soviet juristic opinions on international law are unequivocally for the self-determination of peoples. Let us listen to such opinion:

> International law is a sphere of relentless political struggle whose results have contributed and are contributing to the abolition of colonialism. This struggle shows that very often the political ideas of revolutionary peoples became legal principles of world-wide importance thanks to the active foreign policy of their states. These principles turn into mighty force after they have captivated the minds of the masses and have to be reckoned with by all states, including imperialists. The latter do everything they can to avoid observing international law principles, and very often grossly violate them: however these principles triumph in the end...[52]

The same author also observes "the legitimacy of liberation wars is also recognized in the Declaration of Human Rights which regards it as a last resort."[53] He adds that the Soviet Union and other socialist countries uphold the peoples' right to use any means in their struggle against the colonial yoke, including uprisings, liberation wars, and revolutions. And, national liberation wars being a "means of defence against illegal actions of the colonial powers cannot be qualified as 'acts of internal oppression.' "[54] And again,

> The right of self-defence of states not affiliated with the United Nations is likewise recognized. As the oppressed peoples fighting for liberation, these are, as we have said (above) subjects of international law and as such definitely enjoy the right to self-defence.[55]

In view of the United Nations' deafening silence in the face of history and the legal force behind the Eritrean case, a word is in order regarding the implications of this silence. First, we begin with the assertion that the Eritreans have a valid legal case in their favor. To say that is to recognize the case as passing all tests provided by the rule of recognition sanctioned by the international legal system. In this connection, we must distinguish between legal validity and the *efficacy* of the law in any given situation. As an eminent jurist has written:

> If by "efficacy" is meant that the fact that a rule of law which requires certain behavior is obeyed more often than not, it is plain that there is no necessary connection between the validity of any particular rule and *its* efficacy, unless the rule of recognition of the system includes among its criteria, as some do, the provision (sometimes referred to as a rule of obsolescence) that no rule is to count as a rule of the system if it has long ceased to be efficacious.[56]

As we have seen, the law of nations concerning self-determination is clear and unequivocal. Its nonapplication in the Eritrean case should not, in any way, affect the validity of the Eritrean claim. There has been no evidence of a general disregard of the international law regarding the right to self-determination of colonized peoples. Quite the contrary is the case. And the fact that the system is not generally *efficacious* does not affect its validity.

Eritrea, more convincingly, commands the force of a valid rule of law behind it in its determined resistance against Ethiopia, which violated that rule of law. The armed phase of this resistance has lasted for over a quarter-century. The growth in size and sophistication of the Eritrean Peoples Liberation Front (EPLF) has added further "muscle" to the legal case. The fact that the might of Soviet military power stands behind the Ethiopian adversary invariably led observers to conclude that the Eritrean resistance was finished.[58] This fact of Soviet intervention against Eritrea cries out for comment, at the very least, in view of the USSR's earlier support of Eritrea, and in view of Starushenko's eloquent writing on self-determination. That eloquence now has a hollow ring to it.

The EPLF has successfully repulsed eight major Soviet-backed Ethiopian offensives, since 1978 alone. Each offensive, on the average, involved 98,000 troops, advised by Soviet officers at each brigade level. This gives an idea of the size and capability of the EPLF army, which is no mere guerilla band; its hardware includes tanks, APCs, and heavy artillery, all captured from the Ethiopians.[59]

The EPLF is one step away from acquiring the status of a recognized state. If the present armed conflict results in a stalemate, or in Eritrean victory, or if the United Nations intervenes on the basis of the rightful claim of the Eritreans as argued in this essay, the question of recognition of a new state would come to the fore of the UN agenda. According to Brierly, a new state comes into existence:

... when a community acquires, with a reasonable probability of permanence, the essential characteristics of a state, namely an organized government, a defined territory, and such a degree of independence of control by any other state has to be capable of conducting its own international relations.[60]

In the liberated zone of Eritrea, an efficient machinery of government has been organized by the EPLF with an impressive infrastructure and social services that have earned the puzzled admiration of many independent observers.[61] This zone does not extend to the major cities, such as Asmara, the capital, and their immediate area, although there is public sympathy and support for the EPLF there as well. There would be no question but that the EPLF government services would extend to these occupied areas, after victory or negotiated settlement, whichever comes first. The question of permanence as a criterion of a recognized state in this particular instance is linked to the future of Ethiopia and the performance of the various movements dedicated to its transformation. As for the EPLF's independence from the control of external forces, this has been demonstrated in its history and program of self-reliance.

Paradoxically, despite the legitimacy and legal validity of its claim, the Eritrean case has received until recently less international attention than did Katanga and Biafra. Part of the paradox lies in the fact that the source of the initial successes of both Katanga and Biafra was also the source of their vulnerability. In both cases, there were preexisting provincial ("state") apparatuses (police force, etc.) in addition to the total control of the territory which led to the initial successes. The massive assaults by forces of the central government was met by massive (conventional) defense which led to the defeat and reconquest. As Crawford Young has observed, "a state-based separation is not convertible into a guerilla liberation movement."[62]

By contrast, a guerilla-based operation or a protracted war of liberation can be converted to a state, as the histories of Guinea-Bisau, Angola, and Mozambique have shown. The crucial factors of success are: popular support and high morale stemming from the fact that each fighter is a volunteer prepared to lay down his life. And in the EPLF case, there is an experienced cadre of commanders at the head of a battle-tested liberation army which knows the terrain, as against a relatively inexperienced and ill-motivated army of conscripts. Moreover, the EPLF has become the center of gravity of regional liberation fronts within Ethiopia fighting for varying degrees of autonomy and a democratic restructuring of Ethiopia proper.

In these circumstances, the role of the United Nations in discharging its historic responsibility is clear. That responsibility has been held in abeyance by considerations of geopolitics which reign supreme in its daily functioning. The "hegemony" which the United States enjoyed over the United Nations in 1950, when the fate of Eritrea was decided, has been overshadowed in the last two decades by the emergence of an "alliance" between the "Soviet Bloc" and the "Third World" over a range of issues. But on the issue of the Eritrean people's right to self-determination, when all the facts are placed on the table in the full glare of world public opinion, it would be unlikely for the United Nations to follow a pattern of avoidance of its responsibilities.

NOTES

1. Robert Lansing, Woodrow Wilson's Secretary of State, was among the first to oppose the principle. Robert Lansing, *The Peace Negotiations* (London: Houghton, Mifflin Company, Boston & New York, 1921), p. 87.
2. For more information on the concept of self-determination, see Eisake Suzaki, "Self-Determination and World Public Order: Community Response to Territorial Separation," *Virginia Journal of International Law* 16.4 (Summer 1976):779-862; and Thomas M. Frank and Paul Hoffman, "The Right of Self-Determination in Very Small Places," *New York Journal of International Law* 8.3 (Winter 1976):331-386; Rupert Emerson, *Self-Determination in the Era of Decolonization*, Cambridge: Harvard University Press, Occasional Papers, No. 9, Dec. 1964; Rosalyn Higgins, *The Development of International Law Through the Political Organs of the United Nations*, London: Oxford University Press, 1963; Medard R.K. Rwelamira, "Contemporary Self-Determination and the United Nations Charter," *The African Review*, 6 (1976) 3; Umozurike O. Umozurike, "Self-Determination in International Law," Hamden, CT: Archon Books, 1972.
3. *Charter of the United Nations*, Article 1(2).
4. Ibid., Article 1(4).
5. Ibid., Article 55.
6. G.B. Starushenko, "The Abolition of Colonialism and International Law," *Contemporary International Law*, Ed. by Gregory Tunkin (Moscow: Progress Publishers, 1969), pp. 77-78.
7. Ibid., p. 79.
8. Ibid., p. 79 (emphasis added).
9. Resolution 1514 (xv).
10. Resolution 2160 (xxi) of November 30, 1966.
11. "Preamble," *The Charter of the Organization of African Unity*.
12. Ibid., Article 3.
13. The Declaration of Cairo Conference of the Heads of State and Government, 1964.

14. I.A. Mojoryan, "The Disintegration of the Colonial System of Imperialism and Certain Aspects of International Law," *Soviet Yearbook of International Law*, Moscow (1962), p. 38.
15. "Covenants of Human Rights," *Yearbook of the United Nations*, 1966.
16. Opinion of June 21, 1971 concerning the legal consequence for states of the continued South African presence in Namibia in view of Resolution 250 (1970) of the UN Security Council.
17. Opinion of October 16, 1975.
18. See also Thomas M. Frank, "The Stealing of the Sahara," *American Journal of International Law*, 70 (October 1976):694-721; and Richard A. Falk, "The South West African Case: An Appraisal," *International Organizations* (Winter 1967).
19. Bereket Habte Selassie, "Eritrea and the United Nations," *The Eritrean Case: Proceedings of the Permanent Peoples Tribunal*, Session on Eritrea, May 24-26, 1980, pp. 115-116 (published 1981) which is reproduced in Chapter 2 of the present volume. See also, Tekie Fissehatzion, "The International Dimension of the Eritrean Question," *Horn of Africa*, VI.2:7-24.
20. Selassie and Fissehatzion, Ibid. Also Chapter 2 above.
21. Resolution 390 A(v).
22. See The United Nations Yearbook, 1950, p. 365.
23. See the revealing observations of John Spencer, the then-legal advisor to the emperor's government to the effect: "Both the American and British members of the drafting committee (of the resolution) . . . had particularly stressed to the Ethiopian foreign minister that acceptance by Ethiopia of the provision in the Federal Act (paragraph 13 of Resolution 390 A(v)) requiring its adoption by the Eritrean Assembly would thereby justify termination of the federation upon a concurring vote of that assembly . . ." Spencer advised the then-foreign minister. (For source of the Spencer quote see f.n. 29 of Chapter 2 above.)
24. Order No. 27.
25. In the history of movements for self-government in ex-British Africa, the British used similar stipulation, and "order and good government" as preconditions for the transfer of power to Africans. This subject is dealt with in this author's work, *The Executive in African Governments* (London: Heinemann, 1974).
26. This was clearly stated by the delegate of Czechoslovakia during the debate at the UN General Assembly. For discussion of the validity or non-validity of Ethiopia's precolonial claim, see David Poole, "Ethiopia and Eritrea: The Pre-colonial Period," *The Eritrean Case: Proceedings of the Permanent Peoples' Tribunal*, loc cit., pp. 32-47.
27. Ibid.
28. The Treaty of Ucciale of 1889.
29. See *The United Nations Yearbook*, 1950, p. 365.
30. Proceedings of the Tribunal, loc cit., p. 402.
31. *Review* 26 (June 1981).

32. See Margery Perham, *The Government of Ethiopia* (Oxford University Press, 1973). This expansion was mainly completed at the time of the treaty under which Menelik recognized Italy's colony of Eritrea in 1889. In 1897, it was consummated in a series of treaties which Menelik signed with Britain, among other colonial powers, delineating the southeastern border and incorporating the Ogaden region.
33. Cf. an unpublished paper by Kahsai Berhane, "A Political and Legal Analysis of the Eritrean Question," Brussels, March 29, 1983. The general information is also confirmed by interviews of witnesses present on the occasion, notably by Mr. Tsegay Iyassu, a former lawyer who defended many Eritreans detained for national patriotic activities.
34. The Amharic words are: "Imbi Yalown sow—tiyit agursow."
35. Article 2.
36. See Sir Ivor Jennings, *The Approach to Self-Government* (Cambridge University Press, 1956).
37. Op Cit., p. 392 (emphasis added).
38. *Review*, op cit.
39. Ibid., p. 392.
40. Ibid., pp. 392-393.
41. Article 91.
42. Ibid.
43. *Review*, op cit.
44. The recent capture of Afabet demonstrates the role of the Soviet Union in the provision of arms and personnel.
45. See *External Involvement in Internal Wars*, Ed. by Harry Eckstein (London: The Free Press, 1963), p. 102.
46. *Final Report of the United Nations Commission to Eritrea*, Chapter II, paragraph 201.
47. Article 2(7).
48. See *Horn of Africa*, 4 (1978).
49. Loc cit., p. 404.
50. W.G. Friedman, *Law in a Changing Society* (London: Penguin Books, 1964), p. 87.
51. Ibid., p. 388.
52. Starushenko, op cit., pp. 95-96.
53. Ibid., p. 91.
54. Ibid.
55. Ibid.
56. H.L.A. Hart, *The Concept of Law* (Oxford University Press, 1961), p. 100.
57. Ibid., p. 101.
58. See, for example, Haggai Erlich, *The Struggle for Eritrea* (Hoover Institute Press, 1982).
59. No one now disputes the fact that the EPLF's arms are captured from the Ethiopian army. See f.n. 45 above.
60. J.L. Brierly, *The Law Nations*, 6th ed (Oxford University Press, 1963), p. 137.

61. See Mohamed Abdul-Rahman Babu, "Eritrea: Its Present is the Remote Future of Others," *Africa Events* (October, 1985).
62. Crawford Young, "Comparative Claims to Political Sovereignty: Biafra, Katanga, Eritrea." Paper presented to the Conference on Ethnic Self-Determination and State Coherence: African Dilemmas, Bellagio, Italy, June 8-12, 1981, p. 40.

Chapter 5
The American Dilemma on the Horn

The conflict in the Horn of Africa and its internationalization since 1977 has stimulated many arguments in American policy-making circles on whether the costs of expanded involvement in the region are coming to outweigh the strategic and other benefits.[1] The most intense phase of this controversy has followed the post-1978 realignment of forces in the region, which transformed Somalia into an ally of the United States, and Ethiopia, long a close friend, into a Soviety ally.[2]

The larger debate has sometimes been summed up in terms of two seemingly opposed perspectives in the US foreign-policy establishment: a "globalist" view stressed by those who favor an expanded military presence, and a "regionalist" perspective advanced by those who advocate that American involvement in the region should be oriented primarily towards developmental and humanitarian goals.[3]

Globalists assert that the Horn is strategically important to US interests: (a) to protect the Persian Gulf oil which must pass through sea lanes off the Horn and is thus vulnerable to disruption; (b) to enable America to resupply Israel—a crucial ally—without disruption or delay in the event of a conflict in the Middle East; (c) to counter the Soviet/Cuban presence in Ethiopia since 1977; (d) to help deny the Russians access to the Arabian Sea and thus disrupt their shipping from the Black Sea to the Soviet Far East; and (e) to increase the presence of US nuclear warhead-carrying submarines in an area within range of large parts of the USSR.

Regionalists, on the other hand, fear that American security assistance to countries in the Horn will polarize regional politics, and that the associated use of physical facilities to launch military action in other regions will only widen such crises and drag countries in the Horn—and the United States—into conflicts not of their making nor in their interests. They point to US military assistance to Somalia as having encouraged territorial claims on Ethiopia's Ogaden and Kenya's northern frontier district, and fear that America may be drawn inadvertently into local conflicts between Somalia and its neighbors, thereby identifying the United States in the eyes of Kenya, another local ally, with an aggressor, and so damaging the US diplomatic position on the African continent. They also emphasize that the region's principal needs are developmental and humanitarian, not military. By focusing assistance on such peaceful essentials, they argue, the United States will better advance its regional interests in the long run.

A central, but often neglected, aspect of this debate is the tendency for both globalists and regionalists to underestimate, if not ignore, the autonomy of local, national (or indigenous) social, and political forces in the region. They frequently overstress the power of intervening external actors and factors in both political and economic arenas, whereas their scope and limits in a conflict must be recognized if American policies are to be more realistic and serve the genuine national interests not only of the United States but also of the peoples of the region.

NATIONAL FORCES AND EXTERNAL ACTORS

The conflict in the Horn of Africa is one in which indigenous forces are contending over issues which have complex, historical origins. External powers have intervened on behalf of one or more of the main contestants, particularly in recent years. But the sudden switch of political alliances by Ethiopia and Somalia has deflected the attention of outside observers from the essentially indigenous, internal roots of these regional conflicts. As Palmerston claimed, there are no permanent friends, no permanent enemies, only permanent interests; and this is as true of indigenous social forces as it is in international relations.

What is missing—and hence needed—in discussions of US foreign policy toward the Horn is a greater understanding of the domestic situation, of the historical roots of the region's current political and economic crises. To minimize their importance and lay undue stress on external factors, to force the region's reality into the mechanistic/Manichean context of East-West strategic polarity, is to ignore the objective potency of indigenous social forces. It is to risk perpetuating the erroneous assumption on which America's disastrous policy towards Vietnam was based.

The crisis in the Horn, encompassing several armed conflicts, reflects two interrelated historical processes: (1) a continuing "crisis of empire" within the borders of Ethiopia, a state created through military expansion and the subjugation of national groups in the area from the late nineteenth century onwards; and (2) the persistence of unresolved national and social questions and contradictions shaped by, and inherited from, the European colonial era in Ethiopia, Somalia, and Kenya.

Scope and Limits of Foreign Intervention

There are certain lessons that US foreign policy experts can learn from the Soviet/Cuban intervention on Ethiopia's behalf in 1977-78. Not the least of these is the primacy of indigenous struggles over East-West divisions in shaping the dominant course of events in that region. This external action, as well as the Iranian revolution of 1979 and the Soviet invasion of Afghanistan in 1980, have all underlined the limits of foreign intervention in reshaping local forces.

These events were part of the culmination of a series of local struggles throughout the Third World in the mid- and late-1970s which signalled a changing reality within which the US-Soviet global contention was taking place. While the boldness, speed, and efficiency of Soviet/Cuban action in Ethiopia seemed at first—in contrast to President Jimmy Carter's feeble response to the Iranian crisis—to prove the dominant importance of external over internal forces, in fact this intervention has been unable to suppress or eliminate the historical contradictions between indigenous forces within the region or boundaries of the "empire".

Now power, in terms of military force, and the manner and scale of its use, has always been an important instrument of foreign policy. All the major world powers, not least the United States and the Soviet Union, have inevitably analyzed the use, or potential use, of their military strength when faced with the prospect of promoting or maintaining a given national interest in regard to another country. The manner in which such armed influence is projected is often a product of the technological capability of the big power involved, as well as its attitude towards prevailing norms of international conduct. Such standards constrain governments only to the extent that they have been adhered to by other members of the international community, and they as a whole have become more aware of the limits of military power and the value of restraint and pondered conduct. The risk of nuclear confrontation and the failure of the United States to win the Vietnam war have further sharpened awareness of the limits of external, military action.

The emergence of a group of "non-aligned" countries in the Third World, actively opposed to being ensnared in the web of East-West tensions and desperately seeking to maintain their autonomous definition of the problems they face, has added a new dimension to international relations. That one member of this group, Cuba, which was to preside over the Non-Aligned Movement during 1980-83, became directly involved itself in Ethiopia, reflects the growing complexity of the global scene. What is clear is that the big powers—or their third-world allies or proxies—can no longer expect clear, decisive results from their efforts to sway one or more regional or national situations to serve their interests. These situations retain, despite often massive external intervention, their own indigenous social, political, and economic dynamic.

It is also true, needless to say, that the manner and degree of Soviet and US actions overseas reflect, in turn, their respective domestic policies. Carter's diffident response to developments in Iran, Afghanistan, and Ethiopia was, in great part, a result of the post-Vietnam and post-Watergate climate in the United States. The upcoming election of 1980 also conditioned his responses as Iran, in particular, became a campaign issue itself. Thus any internal conflict overseas, especially if caught up in big power rivalries, may become a factor in the United States which helps to shape the outcome of domestic politics.[4]

Ronald Reagan tried to counter these reverses and repair the damage to America's image when he became president. Through an aggressive posture and strident language, he has sought to prove to friends and foes that America would respond effectively to any challenges to its perceived interests. This was seen most clearly during 1983 in Grenada and in Lebanon. However, in seeking short-term gains in countering what he saw as a "creeping Soviet gain in the Africa crisis," he ignored local realities. The US government's recent preoccupation with opposing perceived Soviet advances risks a harvest of failure in the future as these local realities—unresolved by external intervention—come back to haunt American policymakers in the future.

Where intervention by the Russians has been successful—as in Angola in 1975—it has been so because their external interests have coincided with those of the local people concerned. Certainly the presence of Soviet naval forces in the area, the timely delivery of urgently needed weapons, and the ability to airlift Cuban forces were critical factors. But all this military capability would have come to naught if it had conflicted with the interests of the indigenous Angolan social and political forces resisting the threat of South African occupation.

NATURE AND SOURCES OF THE HORN'S CONFLICT

The conflict in the Horn of Africa is rooted in history and geography. At the heart of the region, and at the center of the several conflicts there, lies the continuing historical reality of an Ethiopian empire that has unified opposing social and national groups within the boundaries still claimed by the regime in Addis Ababa. For the creation and maintenance of that state has meant the continued suppression and exploitation of many non-Ethiopians.

The four central indigenous facets of the conflict in the Horn are: (1) the Ethiopian state, (2) the Eritrean liberation movement, (3) the struggles for self-determination by the people of Tigray (in northern Ethiopia) and of Oromo (in south and southwest Ethiopia), and (4) the Somali-Ethiopian fighting over the Ogaden.

In addition, foreign intervention—to be dealt with later—has not only internationalized and complicated the regional conflict, but has also postponed an earlier resolution by helping the ruling elite in Ethiopia, currently the *Dergue*, to militarize its structures and to resist popular pressures for a peaceful solution.

The Ethiopian State

It is not commonly known that there are two Ethiopias, historically speaking. There is, first, the Ethiopia of ancient records and mythology going back three thousand years, with important political connotations in official Ethiopian accounts. Its starting point in the misty, distant past was the visit by the Queen of Sheba from Northern Ethiopia to King Solomon.[5]

Later Ethiopian Christian scribes, the ideologues of the monarchy, developed local mythology to connect the Ethiopian kings by blood kinship to Solomon, the progenitor of Jesus Christ—all in an effort to further their legitimacy. This legend has been a powerful tool in efforts to preserve the Ethiopian monarchy. Its political implications affected the subsequent development of the Christian Ethiopian state, which started in Axum, in Tigray, and moved southward towards the end of the tenth century. The central state or kingdom has shifted over the centuries from place to place as subsequent rulers sought to avoid being isolated or destroyed. It was based in Gondar during the fifteenth century and changed hands several times before becoming centered in Shoa towards the end of the nineteenth century.

The second Ethiopia is also historical, but shorn of legends. Menelik II of Shoa, who assumed the imperial throne in 1889, was the father of the modern state. After the fall of Axum, Ethiopia was a small highland kingdom with its center limited to the central Shoan, Gondarin, and Tigrayan highlands. The outlying lowlands, including the bulk of the areas inhabited by the Oromo and Somalis today, were not integrated into or ruled by the Christian kingdom.

Menelik II acquired enormous quantities of arms through contacts and astute diplomacy with European colonial powers, and was consequently able to expand his kingdom by conquering the outlying areas south, west, and southeast of Shoa.[6] By the time of the battle of Adua in 1896, when his army defeated the Italians who were invading Tigray from Eritrea, Menelik had conquered and consolidated most of the territories now found within the boundaries of present-day Ethiopia. The people incorporated in this process of conquest include the Oromo, the majority nation in Ethiopia today, as well as the Somalis in the Ogaden. In 1897 Menelik signed a treaty with Britain and France, who formally recognized his conquest and imperial territory. From then on, he was an acknowledged African partner in the era of European colonization. Indeed, his observers had earlier attended the Berlin Conference in 1884-85, which "legalized" the colonial division of Africa.

Menelik is thus seen as a heroic figure for Ethiopians who are proud of this record of conquest. He is a villain, however, to most Somalis, Oromo, and others to whom this "glorious" history was simply the story of their own colonization and loss of national autonomy or self-determination.

Menelik's eventual successor, Haile Selassie, further consolidated this new empire after coming to power as Crown Prince in 1916 and as Emperor in 1930. His supposed "modernization" of Ethiopia, which began in 1931 with the introduction of a European-style constitution, was seen by various national minorities as only "modernizing" their own oppression, since this allowed him further to centralize imperial power. An ultimate irony was that many of the forces that emerged in 1974 to challenge and eventually overthrow the Emperor were products of his modernization efforts—students, teachers, labor unions, and the armed forces.

The military rulers who now control Ethiopia's centralized and still imperial state resemble their predecessors by having been indoctrinated and trained to maintain the empire's territorial integrity as part of a sacred trust. Their adoption of Marxist rhetoric has reinforced rather than challenged this traditional consciousness. They reject the allegations of oppression made by other ethnic groups (or national minorities) by claiming that the ruling class of landlords that formerly oppressed these nationalities has been overthrown, thus eliminating the need for "national" liberation.

It is ironic that Marxism-Leninism—a source of inspiration and useful social analysis for many third-world national liberation movements—has become the rhetorical ideology for maintaining the Ethiopian empire. In "socialist" Ethiopia, class has been posited as the dominant factor over "national" or "ethnic" consciousness. Thus, those who have raised issues of ethnic oppression—for example, the continuing use of Amharic as a national language which puts members of other minorities at a disadvantage in schools and in the government—have been dismissed as "narrow nationalists" or reactionaries. Many, indeed, have been killed for pressing these ethnic concerns.

The central reality of the politics of the Ethiopian state and empire has been, and remains today, the refusal of an imperial elite to share power with other nationalities, even when those were willing to accept the legacy of imperial conquest in return for peaceful and cooperative reconstruction, and some degree of autonomy and democracy. Soon after the "creeping coup" of 1974, however, the Amhara came to dominate the coordinating committee of the armed forces, and once again they have continued the historic pattern of excluding other nationalities from decision-making, in particular the Oromo.

Mengistu Haile Mariam, the leader of the *Dergue*, is an interesting compromise. His culture and upbringing is Amhara, although his parentage is of other minority sources. But the entire structure of the Ethiopian ruling elite—the bureaucracy, the officer corps, and the cabinet—is predominantly Amhara. Mengistu, who admires Menelik, continues to serve the imperial purpose. His slogan, "revolutionary motherland or death," during 1977-78, was instrumental in mobilizing public support for the *Dergue* at a time when the country was at a crossroads—either the continuation of an unreconstructed empire-state, or the real transformation through full, democratic participation of all the people. Mengistu's socialist rhetoric masked his choice of the first option.

The Soviets tragically supported his adoption of this strategy. As a result, they have become allied with an imperial state and are objectively opposed to the national aspirations of peoples demanding self-determination in all parts of Ethiopia. The latter have cogently argued that this stance has undermined the credibility of the USSR's professed motives for intervening. Because a defeat for the Ethiopian elite would represent a disaster for their diplomacy, the Soviets have continued to support a politically and morally bankrupt and increasingly unpopular military junta. The real tragedy is that they have foreclosed any possible role they might have played as conciliators. In Tigray, Oromoland, the Ogaden, and Eritrea, armed struggle seems to be the only means of effectively resolving these contradictions.

The Eritrean Liberation Struggle

The Eritreans have waged a war of national liberation since September 1961, and are a prime example of all the peoples victimized by strategic power manipulation in the post-World War II era. The fact that so few governments have supported the rights of the Eritrean people is a sad commentary on the international community.

The essence of the "Eritrean question" is that a former Italian colony was denied independence contrary to the principles of self-determination recognized by the United Nations since 1945 and by the Organization of African Unity (OAU) since 1963. The coincidence of American geopolitical interests in the region and the demands of Emperor Haile Selassie led to this denial.[7] The Ethiopian regime has continued to label the Eritrean liberation struggle as a secessionist movement that is instigated by outsiders, including some Arab states. The facts speak differently.

Eritrea was a creation of colonial history, like most of today's African states. Italy consolidated its military control during the 1880s, and in 1890 it baptized its colony "Eritrea," having delineated its borders with Ethiopia a year earlier by means of a treaty with Emperor Menelik. Italian rule continued until 1941, when the Allied Forces defeated Mussolini and declared Eritrea a British Protectorate.

For over a decade after that, the Eritrean people were ruled by the British while the future of their country and those of the other former Italian colonies—Libya and Somalia—was the subject of international debate and national agitation after World War II. The UN General Assembly resolved to grant independence to Libya by 1953, and to Somalia by 1960, after a ten-year period of UN trusteeship with Italy as the administering authority. The case of Eritrea proved to be more contentious, because of the insistence by Haile Selassie's regime that the ex-Italian colony should be united with Ethiopia. The Emperor advanced several reasons for making the demand, the main grounds being historical and economic, notably the need for his land-locked state to have access to the sea. Ethiopia's ambitions and American interests in the area prevailed.

In 1950, the United Nations passed a resolution that made Eritrea an autonomous unit "under the sovereignty of the Ethiopian Crown," thereby ignoring the demand of the Eritreans for self-determination.[8] A short time before this decision was implemented in September 1952, John Foster Dulles, the US Secretary of State, bluntly explained the American Government's attitude:

> From the point of view of justice, the opinions of the Eritrean people must receive consideration. Nevertheless, the strategic interests of

the United States in the Red Sea basin and considerations of security and world peace makes it necessary that the country has to be linked with our ally Ethiopia.[9]

A year after the federation had been created between Eritrea and Ethiopia, the latter entered into a 25-year agreement with the United States which lasted until the overthrow of Haile Selassie. In 1962, on the eve of the founding of the OAU, the emperor abolished the federation, incorporating Eritrea into Ethiopia as a Province, in order to prevent the invocation of expected OAU principles in support of self-determination for the people of Eritrea. The growing resistance to Ethiopian rule during the 1960s and 1970s—including the establishment of armed resistance movements—testifies to solid popular commitment to self-determination in the face of international silence on the issue.

The Eritrean Liberation Front grew from a handful of armed bands in 1961 to a sizable, well-armed guerrilla group by 1965. Ethiopian efforts to crush this growing resistance led to massacres which created the first flow of Eritrean refugees into neighboring countries.[10] Although the ELF commanded broad support as a patriotic fighting force, the inability of its leadership to create a really democratic organization led many of the more educated and politically conscious elements in its ranks to form the Eritrean People's Liberation Front in 1970. By 1976, the size of the EPLF had more than quadrupled. Its military predominance was shown by its ability to survive a series of offensives by a much stronger Ethiopian army, first in 1973-74, and again in 1975-76.

The EPLF has a seasoned army which has fought hundreds of battles and has repulsed eight major Ethiopian offensives since 1978. What has been responsible for its success is primarily its widespread popular support, based on its understanding of the social, political, and economic realities of the majority of the people of Eritrea, and also the ingenuity, administrative efficiency, and military capability of its leadership at every level. Outside observers have remarked on its impressive infrastructure and social services—hospitals, workshops, co-operatives, schools—as well as its network of popular organizations for women, youth workers, and farmers.[11]

The Tigrayan and Oromo Liberation Struggles

The Tigray People's Liberation Front represents the latest armed phase of another struggle against the central Ethiopian state. Although Tigray forms part of the highlands of Ethiopia and historically has been part of the empire, resistance to state domination broke out at various times, including in 1943, when a Tigray revolt was suppressed by the emperor with British help. However, the Tigrayans continued to resist, in part through underground activities, and in 1975 formed the TPLF which grew in strength and popularity as it successfully engaged the Ethiopian army. It has organized militia and peasant self-governing bodies, and its land reform and social services in the countryside have improved rural conditions, drawing more support to its side despite Ethiopian efforts to end this "insurgency."[12]

The Oromo Liberation Front is the latest expression of that people's organized opposition to the imperial conquest and rule which was imposed on them by Ethiopia during the nineteenth century. The Oromo are the most populous national group in the central highlands of Ethiopia. Their social structure is based on the *gada* system, a democratic form of social and political organization that ensures participation in public life according to age groups.

Oromo resistance to Ethiopian rule has been sustained since the 1890s in various forms, notably against the confiscation and redistribution of their land among occupying Ethiopians. It was in the mid-1960s that the Oromo organized a qualitative leap forward after decades of simmering revolt and, although their resistance was crushed, they did establish an organizational infrastructure linking students, teachers, civil servants, and even some members of the armed forces and police. The Oromo movement was galvanized by the overthrow of the emperor. Formed in 1974-75, the OLF began launching armed attacks against military outposts, expanding until a new front was opened during 1981 in the western area of Wellega. The split between Christian and Muslim Oromos has impeded more effective campaigns, but these differences are becoming less significant as Oromos fight side by side, reinforcing their national solidarity.[13]

US POLICY TOWARDS THE HORN OF AFRICA

The policy of the United States towards the current crisis in the Horn of Africa is conditioned first by its strategic and geopolitical interests, and second by its perceptions of an aggressive Soviet policy in Africa since 1975 and in the region since 1977. Evidence of American interest in this part of the continent began with the debate among the allies on the "disposal" of the former Italian colonies following the defeat of the Axis powers in 1945, and climaxed in 1980 with the signing of a military agreement between the United States and Somalia.

This period may be divided into three phases: (1) American attempts successfully to step into the shoes of the British; (2) the departure of the latter from Eritrea and the decline of their influence in Ethiopia, illustrated by the signing of the Ethiopia-American treaty on May 23, 1953, albeit ending in February 1977 when the military *Dergue* aligned with the Soviet Union (officially, in November 1978); and (3) the new grouping of forces formalized by the Somali-US agreement of August 1980.

US Policy in the Region: 1945-77

Beginning in the aftermath of World War II and through the end of the 1940s, the United States, in pursuit of its strategic and geopolitical interests in the Horn of Africa, forged an alliance with Ethiopia which it regarded as the most important state in the region. The presence of European colonial powers in neighboring Sudan, Djibouti, and Somalia had precluded earlier American penetration in those areas. As already noted, this strategic concern of the US government and its determination to obtain and maintain a predominant position in the region had been expressed as early as December 1948.

The convergence of US strategic needs with the social and political interests of the ruling Ethiopian elite was articulated most clearly in May 1953 by the 25-year treaty between Ethiopia and the United States that granted the Pentagon use of naval and air facilities and control of a communications base in Asmara, the capital of Eritrea. The treaty formalized what would be the dominant role of the United States in the entire region for the next quarter of a century: Ethiopia was to be the linchpin for anchoring American policy in the Horn among competing European powers. US dominance—which only ended with the demise of Emperor Haile Selassie's regime—was enforced through economic and military aid, as well as by an expanding cultural presence and influence that reinforced its military presence.

Between 1953 and 1977, Ethiopia received some $279 million in American military aid, while 3,552 members of the armed forces were trained in the United States. The Kagnew Communications Center in Asmara was a crucial part of America's worldwide network of linkages that stretched from bases in Morocco to bases in the Philippines. It was used to monitor Soviet activities during the cold war, to gather intelligence in Africa, and especially the Middle East, and clearly played a vital role during both the Korean and Vietnam wars. The development of satellite communications technology, however, and the US decision to expand its presence in the Indian Ocean, reduced the significance of the Kagnew base. By 1976 the number of Americans there had been dropped to 35 from a 1971 peak of 3,000.[14] This led to a progressive decline of military aid.

After the mid-1950s, an increasing amount of US economic assistance was given to Ethiopia, notably in Point Four and later by AID-financed education, health, and agricultural projects. American funds in these sectors gradually came to outstrip military aid. Indeed, by 1977, Ethiopia had received over $350 million in economic assistance, primarily based on the idea of "modernization"—a multi-dimensional concept that included administrative, land, and law reforms, and the progressive opening up of the feudal interior to market forces that were expected to reshape the country and its social forces in line with American conceptions of "development." The overthrow of the emperor and the escalation of struggles for national liberation demonstrated the naivete of these presumptions and how oblivious the donors had been of indigenous realities.

Why did US military and economic aid, though significant by African standards, fail to bring about the expected changes in Ethiopia? There are at least two important reasons. First of all, insufficient priority was placed on developing productive resources and concomitant social changes, thereby leaving intact the historical inequities that fuelled rebellion and resistance to feudal rule. Secondly, the assistance given failed to alter the centralized system whereby all critical decisions were made by the emperor and his hand-picked ministers and governors, leaving intact if not reinforcing traditional antagonisms and the exercise of imperial power. Only after an abortive coup attempt in 1960 did anyone, including the donors, suggest attaching any terms or conditions to aid for Ethiopia.

The US Ambassador to Ethiopia during the 1960s, Edward Korry, expressed this American dilemma in his testimony before the African Affairs Sub-Committee of the Senate in 1976:

> The US interest in Ethiopia was simple then for Washington. The Government defined it as "the unhampered use of Kagnew." The facility was deemed then to be strategically vital to the United States ... the reports on the use of our military aid to Ethiopia were depressing ... and if the Emperor wanted it [i.e., the Kagnew rent money] in a solid gold Cadillac that was his terms and he could have it that way.[15]

The US government made a few efforts to encourage the emperor to introduce some reforms. Although the attempted coup in 1960, and the appointment by President John Kennedy of Korry as Ambassador, had added some urgency and momentum to these efforts, the latter's energetic commitment to "modernization," with its assumption that societies could easily be reshaped from outside with predictable results, did little to speed up needed reforms. The unwillingness of the United States to use its might to press for significant changes in the policies and practices of the

Ethiopian regime effectively linked it to the Emperor's policies. Once Haile Selassie had been overthrown by internal political and economic forces, American influence was to suffer a similar fate.

Korry was assiduous in cultivating contacts among young, influential bureaucrats, organizing seminars on a range of issues and unofficialy hosting meetings of future decision-makers, all the while maintaining an active official dialogue with the emperor and his prime minister. Yet outside this quiet "development diplomacy," the clamor for change was taking on more radical overtones throughout the country. The coup attempt of 1960 was succeeded by organized labor and student demonstrations, and by strikes and revolutionary pamphleteering. Many of the protests were aimed at Korry and the US presence, even as American labor organizations, in cooperation with the International Confederation of Free Trade Unions, were working hard to increase their influence in the newly formed Confederation of Ethiopian Labor Unions. This dual role was to sow the seeds of distrust of US intentions among the emperor and some of his ministers. Looming large in the background of this disintegrating Ethiopian social and political reality was the growing success of the Eritrean liberation movement.

The United States tried to straddle the fence by supporting the emperor while attempting to distance itself from his policies. While trying to identify and control the forces of change, it continued to defend the imperial regime from alleged "communist" subversion. The contradictions of US policy—which subordinated domestic realities to its geopolitical interests—were sharpened by the growing numbers of US Peace Corps volunteers who, because their projects often brought them closer to Ethiopian realities, frequently aligned themselves with the aspirations of these emergent social forces. Some, found helping student protestors, were expelled within 48 hours, further straining US-Ethiopian relations.

Although the attitude of the American government towards the Ethiopian regime began to change (the emperor failed in his 1973 visit to Washington to obtain new jets and tanks), the US commitment to the territorial integrity of the empire, despite the intensifying Eritrean struggle for self-determination, remained unchanged. Growing Soviet assistance to Somalia, including equipment and training for the armed forces, reinforced Washington's support for the anti-communist regime in power in Ethiopia, however unpopular it might be internally.

US Policy in Crisis

The Emperor's failure to alleviate the effects of the 1972-73 famine, despite his power to do so, provoked both international outrage and domestic popular unrest. From this time onwards, American officials vacillated, somewhat leaning towards attempts to disassociate themselves from a regime clearly doomed to fall. The Yom Kuppur war of 1973, which caused Ethiopia to join the other member-states of the OAU in breaking ties with their former ally, Israel, further complicated the geopolitical situation.

The 1974 Ethiopian revolution shook the empire and threw US policy into turmoil. The shadowy coordinating committee which seized power began to articulate a social and political agenda that jolted American expectations. This military group, known as the *Dergue*, was still very much dependent on US aid to the armed forces, given the escalation of the Eritrean war because of the *Dergue's* refusal to resolve this peacefully, and the emergence of more liberation fronts within the empire.

Did the United States still have a serious military interest in Ethiopia in 1975? Although the course of events during the following years seems to support a negative answer, important economic ties were not severed during this period. Indeed, the decision of the American government, until February 1977, was to continue to assist Ethiopia's new regime. Three strategic reasons have been advanced as the basis for his decision. First, if the United States cut off aid, Eritrea would become independent and aligned to the Arab states who could then control both sides of the strategic Bab-al-Mandab, thereby denying Israeli tankers and other vessels access to the Indian Ocean. Second, if Eritrea became independent for lack of American assistance to Ethiopia, it would affect US credibility in the rest of Africa. Third, since the Soviet Union was dominating Somalia and arming its forces, the United States should back Ethiopia as a "regional counterweight" and as guarantee of American credibility.[16]

After some hesitation, US aid was authorized by the secretary of state in February 1975, following a renewed attack by Eritrean guerrillas in the Asmara region. Henry Kissinger (then secretary of state), having discovered Africa via Angola, seems to have insisted that as long as the *Dergue* retained some pro-Western orientation it should be backed, especially in view of the Soviet and Cuban presence in Southern Africa. US policy at that time was expressed by the Assistant Secretary of State, William Schaufele, who told a Congressional committee in August 1976:

> We believe we would incur much criticism from our friends in Africa and elsewhere were we to withdraw support from the Ethiopian Government during this time of difficulty—such a move would also be attributed to distaste for Ethiopia's brand of socialism... Whether we can continue this degree of cooperation with Ethiopia will depend largely on the course finally taken by the new revolutionary regime which assumed power in 1974. It has deliberately decided to

alter Ethiopia's previous reliance on the West, and has consequently strengthened its relations with the Socialist countries. To the extent that this does not lead to systematic opposition to the United States, it still leaves ample opportunity for continued cooperation, particularly as we are sympathetic to many of the new regime's ambitions to improve the living conditions of its people. But the situation is sufficiently volatile to bear close watching.[17]

This is a level-headed Palmerstonian view, made by a spokesman of a Republican administration in the face of some opposition to further aid to the new regime from the American right-wing for traditional anti-Soviet reasons, and from liberals who condemned continued repression in Eritrea and within Ethiopia.[18]

Washington continued to be guided not by an understanding of the brewing social contradictions within Ethiopia, but by broader external factors such as the global confrontation with the Soviet Union. As the *Dergue*'s ties with Moscow grew, so did pressure for the United States to stop aid to Ethiopia. Although the Carter administration was to invoke human rights as the reason for ending aid to the *Dergue*, its willingness to arm a not much more progresive Somalia and Sudan—once they had expelled their Soviet advisers in 1977—reflected the continuation of an historical tendency to evaluate events along predetermined lines for their effect on US world interests, rather than on the civil and social rights of the majority of people still under the rule of the *Dergue*.

A Changing US Policy: 1977 to the Present

In February 1977, Mengistu Haile Mariam emerged as the leader of the *Dergue*, having eliminated many rivals and having increased urban repression by massacring those who had protested against his use of violence to advance his own position. The Carter administration quickly announced that it would suspend all aid because of violations of human rights; the *Dergue* responded by closing all American installantions in April 1977, except for the embassy and the AID office. The US government soon halted the delivery of previously ordered weapons, and announced its intention of selling arms to two neighboring governments, both of which had been accused by the *Dergue* of supporting the liberation movements within Ethiopia—namely, the Sudan in Eritrea and Somalia in the Ogaden —that the Americans had·previously helped the Ethiopian military to suppress.

The use of human rights as the rationale for cutting off aid to Ethiopia was, in reality, more of a pretext than a true basis for that decision. The switch by Washington to supporting the Sudan and Somalia was primarily a response to changing political and military developments in the region, thereby altering the balance of strategic advantage *vis-a-vis* the USSR. Of primary concern to the United States was the interest shown by Saudi Arabia in weaning Mogadishu away from Moscow's influence and back to the "Islamic fold." The alienation of Somalia from the Soviet Union because of the latter's growing ties with Ethiopia, combined with the *Dergue*'s expulsion of US military personnel, reinforced the convergence of Saudi and American interests.

US-Somali Relations

In looking at the alliance that emerged after 1977 between America and Somalia, it is crucial to understand the nature and source of the latter's claims and motives in the region. Until 1977, the interests of the United States had always led it to back Ethiopia as regards autonomy for the Ogaden, and to turn down Somali requests for military aid in the early 1960s as a possible threat to the security of the emperor. The creation of the OAU in 1963, and the adoption of the Cairo Resolution in 1964 accepting the inviolability of colonial boundaries, reinforced this American position.

There are three issues intertwined in the "Ogaden question:" (1) the border dispute between two sovereign states, Ethiopia and Somalia, over boundaries left undemarcated by Ethiopia and Italy; (2) the Somali claim to "Western Somalia," including the Ogaden and sections of the Haud and Bale; and (3) the right to self-determination of the people of these territories as expressed in the struggle of the West Somali Liberation Front. Although the United States has consistently rejected the WSLF as an extension of Somali territorial claims, it has taken no firm position on the border dispute, supporting an amicable settlement.

The unification of the former British and Italian Somalilands in 1960 created one of Africa's few authentic "nation-states," its people sharing a common language, culture, history, and religion (Islam). Contemporaneously, however, large numbers of ethnic Somalis inhabited the Haud Ogaden and Bale Provinces of imperial Ethiopia, as well as the northern frontier district of Kenya and parts of Djibouti. This demographic reality helps to explain the persistence of the "Ogaden question," although the following factors are also important: (a) the history of resistance by the Somali people against alien occupiers goes back to 1897; (b) the former colonial power, Britain, promised after World War II to create a pan-Somalia that would embrace the present-day state and large segments of the Ogaden, Haud, and Northern Kenya; (c) the growth of "irredentist" movements in these areas after the 1950s meant that many were seeking to reunite with Somalia; (d) the transformation of the WSLF from an "irredentist" into a liberation movement meant demanding self-determination first before any decision was taken about whether or not to reunite with Somalia or to remain within Ethiopia as an autonomous region, thereby creating tensions and muted recriminations between the mainstream WSLF elements and those who opt for unconditional union with Somalia; and (e) the history of the Ethiopian repression of the Ogaden included restrictions on the free movement of traditionally nomadic people and on their access to water and grazing, thus feeding the continuing conflict.

Wars have been fought between Somalia and Ethiopia, first in 1960 and again in 1964. The following year, the regime in Mogadishu sent pilots to the USSR for training and strengthened its ties with Moscow, all the while increasing the size of its army. President Siad Barre, who seized power from the civilians in 1969, had more than doubled his armed forces by 1976, having signed a Treaty of Friendship with the USSR two years previously. Soviet military advisers played an important role until around the time of the Somali intervention in the Ogaden during 1977, when the regime changed alliances and expelled most of them.

The 1977-78 war marked a significant realignment of forces in the region. It was affected by several other developments, including: (a) the suspension of US military aid to Ethiopia; (b) the mutual defense pact between Egypt and the Sudan, following the abortive coup attempt in 1976 against President Gaafar Muhammad Numeiri with alleged Libyan and Ethiopian assistance; (c) the US agreement to supply Kenya with twelve F-5 jets; (d) Sudan's expulsion of Soviet advisers in 1977; and (e) Ethiopia's growing ties with the USSR.

The Somalis were dismayed by the continued American refusal to send them arms after their invasion of the Ogaden, given Soviet and Cuban support for Ethiopia in the conflict, and the initial success of the WSLF advances in the Ogaden itself. In late 1977, Somalia broke its treaty with the USSR and expelled all Soviet advisers. By then, those units of the national army supporting the WSLF were suffering serious defeats at the hands of the Ethiopians who had been newly equipped and trained by the USSR and who were aided by Cuban troops. By March 1978, Somalia withdrew its troops from the Ogaden, though it continued to support the WSLF guerrilla struggle as before.

Washington was preoccupied during this period with devising means of thwarting an Ethiopian invasion of Somalia and preventing the overthrow of the Siad Barre regime in favor of one more closely aligned with the Soviet Union. The US Secretary of State, Cyrus Vance, warned in February 1978 that America might decide to provide military aid to Somalia if Ethiopia invaded its neighbor. The *Dergue* responded by charging that the United States was already doing that by supplying arms to Somalia through Iran, Pakistan, Spain, and Saudi Arabia.

Siad Barre remained in power during these critical years, despite predictions to the contrary. However, the remarkable gains in development achieved during 1969-75 were thrown into question by the diversion of most national resources to meet the survival needs of the huge inflow of refugees from the Ogaden, by the mismanagement of revenue, and by the allocation of vast funds to sustain internal and external security. Human rights violations reportedly rose as Siad Barre sought to stifle Somali protests over the outcome of this adventure.[18]

In part because he was able to survive, Siad Barre eventually came belatedly to reap the fruits of American realignment towards Somalia. In 1978, The United States had as a precaution sent a naval task force to the Indian Ocean and the Red Sea, and the Assistant Secretary of State for African Affairs, Richard Moose, had visited Mogadishu to discuss the possible supply of defense weapons. By then the United States had begun to accept the *fait accompli* of a consolidated Soviet presence in Ethiopia, consummated by a Treaty of Friendship in late 1978 which included provisions for military aid.

By 1979, the United States was moving towards signing an agreement that would allow access to Somali ports and airfields in return for financial and military assistance. This shift in policy occurred against a background of regional events problematic to US interests, notably (a) a new Ethiopian offensive in the Ogaden, setting off further waves of refugees fleeing into Somalia, coordinated with a fresh offensive in Eritrea,[19] and (b) an appeal by newly independent Djibouti for help in defending itself against an alleged Ethiopian plot to overthrow its leaders.

Washington responded by sending an aircraft carrier into the Indian Ocean to underscore American concerns in the region, and such projections of power continued into 1980.

The US-Somali Agreement: New Ally, Old Naivete

The agreement between the United States and Somalia cemented the new alliance between the two Governments, after written assurances had been given to satisfy Congress that American weapons would not be used in the Ogaden. Some 250 US military personnel were sent to Somalia as part of the November-December 1980 "Operation Bright Star" military manoeuvers in the Middle East.[20]

In the financial year 1982, the US Defense Department proposed to sell $42 million worth of "defensive" military equipment to Somalia, while the

US Navy suggested an expenditure of $24 million for port and airfield expansion, and $400,000 for refurbishing the facilities at Berbera. Concurrently, the United States expected to provide $20 million in development assistance and $25 million in food aid. In the wake of Ethiopian offensives in the Ogaden and across the border in support of Somali dissident forces, the Barre regime asked for more aid, and Congress approved an additional $5 million under a supplemental appropriations bill. The Reagan administration's foreign aid proposal for the financial year 1983 called for a $1 million drop in economic help and a $10 million increase in security assistance.[21]

Reagan and the US-Soviet Strategic Struggle

As Tom Farer has observed,

> When the Soviets were ensconced in Somalia, NATO governments tended to associate their presence there primarily with the seaborne threats to Western interests in the Indian Ocean and its littoral. Without diluting that concern, the Soviet shift into Ethiopia has uncovered additional and more intensely threatening vistas.[22]

The Reagan administration brought to Washington an intensified fear of growing Soviet influence in the region. This "globalist" perspective, somewhat softened and modified under the Carter administration by its concern for human rights and its awareness of indigenous sources of conflict in Africa, sharpened anew under the focus of Reagan's rigidly anti-Soviet policy prism. The continued role of Cuban forces in Angola and Ethiopia intensified anxiety in the United States that Ethiopia would be "converted into an armory, conference center, training ground and military sanctuary for dissidents."[23]

The USSR has certainly demonstrated its determination to keep the Mengistu-dominated *Dergue* in power. Hence, American fears for the instability of pro-Western regimes, such as that of Nimeiri (of the Sudan) bordering on Ethiopia, have grown with the role of Soviet advisers and military aid.[24] However, others in the Washington policy establishment have continued to argue that the USSR has its own regional interests that militate against adventurist attempts to overthrow neighboring governments that might end in failure and expulsion.

The fact that the Soviet Union is bogged down in armed conflicts within Ethiopia is, of course, regarded by the United States as a not altogether unmitigated disaster; the US hoping perhaps that Eritrea will prove to the the USSR's Vietnam-type quagmire. Yet America has held back direct aid for the Eritreans since their radical social programs not less than their fierce sense of autonomy of policy and action put them at odds with US regional allies and with US hopes for eventually reshaping the Horn of Africa to other economic and political designs.

And, in part, the United States may expect to be able to "retrieve" Ethiopia from Soviet dominance, for the following reasons: (a) although an increasing number of African states are helping the Eritreans, the *Dergue*'s position on the "question of nationalities" is generally supported by the OAU; (b) Ethiopia has more valuable resources than Somalia and is of equal if not greater strategic importance; (c) there are still many social forces within Ethiopia strongly favoring reassociation with the West for political, economic, and cultural reasons; (d) the *Dergue*'s nationalism far outweighs its "proletarian internationalism" when it comes to concrete policies and programs; (e) the USSR has proved to be no better than the United States in resolving the socio-economic and political contradictions of Ethiopia represented by the continued wars of liberation in Eritrea, the Ogaden, Tigray, and Oromoland, while the economic models for a "non-capitalist road to development" have produced few results; and (f) the USSR has been unable to help the *Dergue* win the war in Eritrea and elsewhere, creating disaffection and recrimination, and leading to growing desertions.

This continuing ambivalence in Washington's policy towards Ethiopia is shown by the fact that it has not actively opposed loans from multilateral institutions such as the International Monetary Fund and the World Bank, in contrast to its intransigent opposition to similar assistance to Vietnam and Nicaragua. However, it has continued to strengthen Somalia's defense capability, increasing its aid in 1982 and 1983 to counter growing Ethiopian attacks on Somali territory, as well as the *Dergue*'s agreement with Libya and South Yemen on financial aid.[25]

The dilemma facing US policymakers who desire to "regain" Ethiopia is that military manoeuvers designed to strengthen their allies in the region—such as Egypt, the Sudan, and Somalia—may have the effect of increasing Ethiopian and Libyan reliance on Soviet support. A constant argument heard in Mogadishu for more military aid is that the other side is armed to the teeth with offensive weapons, making Somalia ever-vulnerable to aggressive attacks.

CONCLUSIONS

What can we conclude from this review of US policy options and decisions? The following points are the most significant:

First, the Horn of Africa remains of great strategic value to America and its allies, its importance not having diminished despite the reduced need for a communications center there.

Second, US policy in the Horn has been conditioned by US general geopolitical and strategic interests in the region, and within the African continent as a whole. The Soviet-Cuban intervention in Angola in 1976 and Ethiopia in 1977 came as shocks to Washington. They were interpreted—despite the brief period of early Carter administration concern with human rights—as clear expressions of growing Soviet aggressiveness, rather than as essentially indigenous, internal social conflicts which remained unresolved by prior external aid policies of the United States, and which the Russians took advantage of but did not create themselves. The Reagan administration has abandoned any niceties represented by the "regionalist" approach, and has placed the Horn squarely in the context of East-West confrontation, decisively breaking from the Carter administration's attempt to recognize and respect African attempts to define their own needs of self-determination, territorial integrity, and progress in economic development.[26]

Third, recent American actions have remained primarily reactive to external, not internal, factors. They have been guided by responses to real or perceived Soviet expansion, moves that have taken place against the background of momentous changes in Africa as a whole. In neglecting the indigenous roots of most of these developments, the United States is increasingly viewed by a number of African leaders as opposing such changes and even trying to reverse many of them. This is perhaps most clear in southern Africa; but in the Horn, the US dilemma is made more acute by the range and complexity of the conflicts and social contradictions in the region. Torn between supporting what appeared to be an expansionist Somalia and adherence to OAU principles of respecting the status of boundaries, the United States has been guided less by respect for national identity than by a short-sighted approach to its interests in the region. The Soviets have been equally insensitive to self-determination, albeit more decisive in supporting their ally of the moment, militarily. The growing US assertiveness *vis-a-vis* Libya and support for the Sudan may intensify and not diminish the dangers of a regional escalation of the conflict.

Fourth, the hostilities in the Horn have been conditioned by the continued reality of the Ethiopian empire, by the unresolved national struggles in the region, by the outstanding colonial question posed by Eritrea, and by the continuing Ethiopian-Somali struggle over the Ogaden. However, these problems have been compounded, not moved towards resolution, by the tendency of US policymakers to internationalize the causes of the conflict.

Fifth, colonial history, as in the case of Eritrea, forges a national consciousness and a series of socio-economic formations that cannot be ignored or suppressed. Thus, foreign policy that ignores that reality—for example, by the United States from 1953-77, and by the USSR from 1977 to the present—will eventually founder on the inability of external inputs to restructure what has been built up from indigenous history. External inputs are essentially secondary in their impact. They can have important effects (such as stopping the South African advance in Angola in 1975, or the Somali successes of 1977-78), but they cannot be decisive in defeating mass popular will and support, although they may lead to greater loss of life. And the dependence of regimes on external forces that continue to prop them up (Barre on the United States, the *Dergue* on the Soviet Union), far from making the situation more tractable for external powers, may set in motion social forces that undermine their credibility and stability.

Sixth, military adventures are no substitute for political solutions. Lebanon bears eloquent, if tragic, testimony to this fact. The continued inability of Ethiopia to impose a military "solution" on the Eritrean conflict, despite aid from the United States from 1953-77 and from the Soviet Union from 1977 onwards, is a cogent example.

Finally, the future of the Horn of Africa may be predicted more accurately by a careful analysis of the mass popular movements—and the new institutions, politics, and culture they are creating and consolidating—rather than by any study that focuses on the shifting strategic interests of external powers. It is only possible to understand the changing alliances of the region by analyzing class, ethnic, and national divisions created over time.

NOTES

1. This question has defined the terms of the debate since early 1976. See, for example, "Ethiopia and the Horn of Africa," hearings before the Subcommittee on African Affairs of the US Senate Foreign Relations Committee, Washington, D.C., 1976.
2. See Harry Brind, "Soviet Policy in the Horn of Africa," in *International Affairs*, London, 60.1 (Winter 1983/4):75-95.
3. See "The Horn of Africa and the United States," Issue Brief No. 1B78019, Library of Congress Research Service, October 22, 1982.
4. "America Held Hostage" was the title of a continuing series of nightly reports and commentaries on one of the top national TV networks (ABC), lasting for

several months during 1980, following the seizure of American hostages by the Khomeini regime.
5. The *"Kabra Nagast"* ("Glory of Kings"), authored by royal scribes, tells the story of the supposed journey by the Ethiopian Queen of Sheba to behold the wisdom of Solomon, who artfully seduced his unsuspecting visitor after being overcome by her beauty. Menelik I was claimed as the offspring of that union.
6. Margery Perham, *The Government of Ethiopia*, London: Faber and Faber, 1948.
7. More evidence has come to light to substantiate such a collusion, thanks to the US Freedom of Information Act. Examples are letters written by the Defense Secretary, James Forrestal, to the Secretary of State, Dean Acheson, on December 11, 1948, indicating support for Emperor Haile Selassie's claim over Eritrea in return for the grant of strategically important naval and air facilities in Massawa and Asmara.
8. For a detailed discussion, see Chapter 4 for the content of the letter.
9. Cited in Linda Heiden, "The Eritrean Struggle for Independence," *Monthly Review* 30.2 (June 1978):15.
10. By 1982, this flow had grown ten-fold to over 500,000, most living in the Sudan.
11. Among these are Dan Connell, representing (earlier) *The Washington Post*, and (later) *The Guardian* (London), *Le Monde* (Paris), and Reuters (London); Guido Bimbi, representing some left-wing Italian papers; Gérard Chaliand and Jean-Louis Peninou of *Libération* (Paris), and Mary Dines of War on Want (London). Several films have also been made depicting life in the liberated areas.
12. Equally ominous to the *Dergue* is the emergence of a TPLF-supported, all-Ethiopian fighting front called the Ethiopian Peoples Democratic Movement, now operating in the central Province of Wollo and parts of Begemidar (Gondar). The EPDM is also recognized by the EPLF, and aims to replace the *Dergue* with a democratic government.
13. The Tigrayan People's Liberation Front and the Oromo Liberation Front have recognized each other. See statements made by the TPLF central committee member, Asfaha Kahsai, in *Horn of Africa* (Summit, NJ, IV.3, 1981), and by the OLF central committee member, Ahmed Buna (Ibid., III.3, 1982). Although no statement has yet been made about how the OLF views the EPDM and *vice versa*, the latter organization recognizes the right of any nationality to self-determination and, hence, presumably Eritrea's right to independence. The EPDM's first Congress, held in Derbie, Northwest Ethiopia, was attended by a central committee member from the EPLF, as revealed in its newsletter, *Eritrean Bulletin*, Paris 2.31 (December 1983).
14. See Fred Halliday and Maxine Molyneux, *The Ethiopian Revolution* (London: NLB, 1981) pp. 215-16.
15. See "Ethiopia and the Horn of Africa," Hearings Before the Sub-Committee on African Affairs on the US Senate Foreign Relations Committee, Washington, D.C., 1976.

16. Tom J. Farer, *War Clouds on the Horn of Africa: The Widening Storm* (Washington, D.C.: Carnegie Endowment for International Peace, 1976), p. 151. See also Halliday and Molyneux, op. cit., p. 220.
17. See Hearings Before the Sub-Committee on African Affairs of the US Senate Foreign Relations Committee.
18. For example, US Congressman, Howard Wolpe, voiced such criticism as Chairman of the House Sub-Committee on Africa. *Congressional Record*, V.128, (August 18, 1982).
19. By 1980, the number of Somali refugees had reached the million mark according to a report by the United Nations High Commission for Refugees (UNHCR). In Eritrea the ill-fated 5th offensive began around this rime, sending new waves of Eritrean refugees to the Sudan, which number some 500,000 according to the UNHCR.
20. Wolpe, loc. cit.
21. Ibid. The US response to this Somali appeal included communications equipment, anti-tank weapons, light arms, and ammunitions worth at least $20 million according to a survey of the Institute of International and Strategic Studies for 1982-83.
22. Tom Farer, "Soviet Strategy and Western Fears," *Africa Report*, Washington (November-December 1978).
23. Ibid.
24. Fears of such instability have revived with the emergence of the Sudan Peoples Liberation Movement, a rebellion in Southern Sudan which the Numeiri regime claimed is trained and assisted by the *Dergue* and Libya's Muammar Qadhafi. Recent military activities include kidnapping and killing of personnel of the US oil corporation Chevron. Numeiri's decree to extend Islamic law to the South had added fuel to the fire, and finally led to his downfall.
25. According to *The Economist*, London, February 13, 1983, US military aid for 1982-83 amounted to $65 million, with more promised for 1983-84. But no tanks or aircraft have yet been forthcoming, in accordance with the American policy of providing Somalia with defensive weapons only.
26. According to Brind, loc cit., p. 95, "Soviet leverage, formerly in Somalia, now in Ethiopia, was and is limited. To remain in either country against the wishes of its government, even if that were possible, would undermine its position in Africa and in the Third World generally."

Chapter 6

The World Bank: Power and Responsibility in Historical Perspective

The World Bank has become a subject of controversy, of learned discourse, and of endless debate between the Left and the Right. The Bank has become the foremost multilateral, international lending agency, with an expanding role covering a variety of sectors and involving billions of dollars' worth of loans to the Third World, on terms not available from commercial banks.

As its role expanded, the Bank began to draw increasing attention, both favorable and critical. The London *Economist* recently called it "a bank for all seasons." It is viewed differently by different people, depending on their ideological positions or perspectives. These perspectives may be reduced to two basic positions, divided along a Left/Center and a Center/Right axis.

The Left critique has found the Bank—on its record—an instrument of Western corporate capital.[1] The thrust of the Leftist argument is that the Bank has not proved useful to the great mass of Third World peoples, and that the ruling elite of its borrowing countries have derived benefits from its lending activities. The argument also holds that multinational corporations stand behind its activities, also benefitting by selling their goods, which are not basic necessities to ordinary people.

The Centrist position is essentially supportive of the Bank's role as an important vehicle for the transfer of resources for development of the

Third World and as a facilitator of trade among nations.[2] The numerous publications financed or sponsored by the Bank itself fall into this category. Their wealth of information provides an insight into the Bank's philosophy and into many aspects of its diverse activities. At the same time they may also be regarded as organizationally self-serving.

The second level of controversy, running along a Center/Right axis, is relevant today in the context of "Reaganomics." The Right is represented in the budget-cutters of the Reagan administration, who view foreign aid as wasteful. David Stockman, the former director of the Office of Management and Budget (OMB), for example, has charged that the International Development Association (an affiliate of the Bank) has not used its leverage to redirect Third World economies towards a market orientation. The Liberal (Center) answer to the Rightist assault on the Bank has been to say that the Bank promotes economic growth, domestically by stimulating capital accumulation through savings and investment, and externally through export expansion and diversification.[3]

To this must be added what may be called a Third World perspective, which is not reducible to a single ideological category because it is a composite of different ideologies. Its unifying theme is a sense of a historical wrong committed against the Third World, a wrong that has yet to be rectified. Movements towards rectification converged in a demand for a new and more just international economic order (NIEO), which was given a stamp of legitimacy when the UN General Assembly passed a resolution adopting some NIEO demands in 1975.[4] One aspect of the demand is that there should be an equitable representation in the governance of the Bretton Woods institutions: the International Monetary Fund (IMF) and the World Bank. This paper deals with an aspect of governance in the World Bank: management and decision-making and its relationship to the structure and origin of the Bank.

THE POLITICAL ECONOMY OF GOVERNANCE

The World Bank operates within the framework of a system established at the close of World War II at Bretton Woods, New Hampshire, by the dominant forces of the world economy, led by the United States of America. The IMF was mandated under its charter to provide short-term loans to help member countries facing balance of payment deficits and to enforce financial discipline in a post-war international financial system.[5] Its role has often been portrayed as that of policeman of the international financial order. The metaphor is helpful in apprehending the reality which is not always immediately apparent.

The World Bank, on the other hand, was mandated to help finance reconstruction after the war, and to foster development efforts through the transfer of resources.[6] Out of Bretton Woods also came the General Agreement on Tariff and Trade (GATT) designed to help regulate trade, although it had less success. Then, in 1964, the United Nations Conference on Trade and Development (UNCTAD) was founded at the behest of the Third World countries which had, by then, started expressing a growing dissatisfaction with the Bretton Woods system. Using UNCTAD as a forum, the Third World countries (known as "South") articulated concerns on questions of terms of trade. From UNCTAD I (1964) to UNCTAD IV (1972) the "South" emerged sufficiently united to make concrete demands. As already noted, the South was backed, after 1973, by the oil power of the OPEC States. Running parallel to this development was a wealth of theoretical works on the nature and priorities of development by a number of authors, many Third World economists among them (for example, Samir Amin, Walter Rodney, and the European Andre Gunder Frank, etc.). All of these launched the theoretical equivalent of NIEO, attacking the conventional wisdom on the economics of growth.

The decline of OPEC's power since then, the resistance of the "North," and a subsequent downturn in the world economy have negated much of the momentum gained and epitomized in NIEO which seems to have run out of steam. But the "North-South" dialogue continues. The North continues to export capital and manufactured goods and services, while the South exports raw materials, and (in some cases in recent years) manufactured and semi-processed goods produced through the employment of cheap labor. Historically, this "division of labor" was characterized by unequal rates of growth and exchange—high rates of growth in the North and very slow rates of growth in the South. In the quarter-century between the end of World War II and 1973, the North enjoyed a rate of growth unparalleled in recorded history, while the gap between North and South grew wider. Moreover, and despite the unparalleled economic growth in the North, the world economy was subject to periodic crises and failures to meet the basic needs of a large proportion of the world population.[7]

The place and role of the World Bank in this scheme of things continues to be of interest. The Bank reflects the world economic system in a number of ways, notably in its structure, philosophy, and lending practices. Its governance, and management policy and style, is a crucial aspect of its role. The Bank is also a sister institution of the IMF. Indeed, the architects of the Bretton Woods system made certain that membership in the International Bank for Reconstruction and Development (IBRD) (the backbone of the World Bank group) was conditioned upon membership in the IMF.[8]

Finally, it must be noted that two affiliates were added to the IBRD, together now making up the World Bank group. In 1955, the International Finance Corporation (IFC) was established to further the growth of private enterprise in member countries through direct investment in companies established on private enterprise principles. Then in 1960, the International Development Association (IDA) was established to provide finances to member countries on easier terms—interest-free and fifty year payment schedules.

CAPITAL STRUCTURE AND GOVERNANCE

The IBRD was established with an authorized capital of $10 billion (in 1944 US dollars) divided into $100,000 portions and made available for subscription by members. As of 1984, the authorized capital had been increased to $86 billion, following a selective capital increase authorized in 1977. Of the originally subscribed capital, ten percent, or about $1 billion, was actually paid into the bank and has been used and is usable for the most part in Bank operations. The remaining 90 percent, equal to $9 billion, is "uncalled" and can be employed only to meet the obligations of the Bank to holders of it securities. US money markets were the principal source of the Bank's operational funds which it obtained through bond issues. The subscriptions of IDA and IFC were not sufficient for lending operations. They depended on the IBRD. IDA funds now come mostly from government sources. Discussions have been held recently with a view to a further increase in the capital to $93 billion.

From the start the largest shares were held by the United States, followed by the United Kingdom and France, and later by West Germany and Japan. Out of IBRD's total initial subscription of $9,100 million, the United States, the United Kingdom, and France along had more than half of the shares of capital: $3,175 million, $1,300 million, and $45 million, respectively. With the increase in the Bank's membership, the percentages began to change.

In 1970, the combined US-UK-France capital share had been reduced to 43.18 percent of the total, and to 36.75 percent by 1980. If we add Germany and Japan, the combined share of the five industrialized countries in 1980 amounted to 48.07 percent of the total. What implications does this have on the governance and policy of the Bank?

To begin with, the Bank's Articles follow the usual corporate system of weighted voting, under which the largest shareholders control the votes. In the case of the Bank, however, there is a slight difference. The 48.07 percent share of the five countries noted above, for instance, would have 43.59 percent of the total voting power of the member countries. This anomaly has a statutory basis, in that the Articles predicated voting rights on: (1) a fixed number of (250) of "membership votes" and (2) additional votes for each share of stock held, at the rate of one vote per $100,000 (1944) subscription. Thus, each member has 250 votes, plus one additional vote for each share of stock held.[10]

This structure of weighted voting has the effect of bringing some divergence, as noted above, between the percentage of the capital share owned by a member and the percentage of its voting power. In the example cited earlier for instance, when the US capital share in 1970 was 27.42 percent of the total, its voting power was 24.51 percent; the combined US, UK, and French cpaital share for that year was 43.18 perecent, while their combined voting power was 38.77 percent. Again, in 1980, the addition of Germany and Japan raised this combined capital share to 48.07 percent, while the voting power was 43.59 percent of this total. For a controlling majority vote in 1980, three other industrialized countries were needed: Canada (3.39 percent), the Netherlands (2.36 percent), and Belgium (2.24 percent). This would bring the total to 51.58 percent.

It is often stated in Bank circles that the weighted voting system has no "ostensible function"; decisions by the board of executive directors are mostly unanimous.[11] It is claimed, somewhat illogically, that the statutory presence of the system has been indispensable to the scale of the Bank's operations, and that without it the Bank would not have been entrusted with the resources it now has at its disposal. The claim is illogical only in relation to the point that the weighted voting system has no ostensible function. It has a function, if not an ostensible one. Such a function flows logically from its role as a silent guarantor of the basic policy of the dominant forces in the world system. The fact that the voting right has not been exercised is a reflection of many considerations, principal among them being the fact that the industrialized countries of the North are the providers of the funds and the countries of the South are the borrowers.

From the capital-exporting North's point of view, it would go against its basic policy if decisions in the Bank were to be delayed or hamstrung, and loan operations suspended. Such an eventuality would come if the Southern members were to be constantly frustrated and had to resort to confrontation tactics. On the other hand, the borrowing states need financial resources to buy equipment, to mention one obvious example, and their comparative weakness in the voting structure leads to an apparent mutuality of interests. All that is needed then is an able management led by a president steering delicately through the complex web of interests. We will examine the role of the president of the Bank in the decision-making process after we consider the functions of the Board of Governors and executive directors in the Bank's decision-making process.

THE BOARD OF GOVERNORS

The power of the Bank is legally vested in the Board of Governors consisting of one governor and one alternate appointed by each member country. These serve for five years or more, subject to the pleasure of the appointing member. The alternate votes only in the absence of the Governor. The Board may delegate to the executive directors authority to exercise any of its powers, with the exception of seven matters.[12]

1. admission of new members;
2. increase or decrease of capital stock;
3. suspension of a member;
4. decisions on appeals from interpretations of the Articles of Agreement by the executive directors;
5. making long-term arrangements to cooperate with other international organizations;
6. decisions to suspend permanently the operation of the Bank and distribute its assets; and
7. determination of the distribution of the net income of the Bank.

The board meets annually and selects a chairman to serve for one year. Special meetings may be called either by the board itself or by the executive directors whenever five members of the Bank, or a member or members having more than a quarter of the total voting power, so request. Such a request must be made through the executive directors and communicated by the president of the Bank, as chairman of the board of executive directors.

The board of governors has delegated a wide range of powers to the executive directors, with the exceptions noted above. Its function may thus appear to be a mere formality, acting as a legitimatizing rubber stamp for decisions made by the executive directors and the management; but it can serve, and has served, as an international public forum for the expression of opinions and for taking a stand on important issues that need publicity. The entire policy of the Bank is theoretically open to review at the annual meeting of the board of governors. In practice, the occasion has been used as a safety valve for venting pent-up feelings and frustrations, and to a certain extent for some "horse trading." The governors are usually ministers of finance or heads of central banks, for whom the occasion provides a kind of clearinghouse for financial information. Delicate financial matters are discussed and views are exchanged informally.[13]

THE EXECUTIVE DIRECTORS

The general operation of the Bank is conducted by the executive directors who exercise all powers delegated to them by the board of governors. The foregoing discussion of voting rights is therefore primarily related to voting at meetings of the executive directors, who perform their duties on a full-time basis at the Bank's headquarters in Washington, D.C. For all practical purposes, the executive directors, not the board of governors, are the *formal* decision-makers of the Bank. They decide on all loan proposals submitted to them by the President of the Bank, and on broad policy matters within the framework of the Articles of Agreement. They present to the Board of Governors, at its annual meeting, an audit of accounts, an administrative budget, and an annual report, discussing the operations and policies of the Bank, plus any other matter that in their judgment requires submission to the Board.

The Articles of Agreement provide for twelve executive directors, of whom five are appointed (one by each of the five members having the largest number of shares) and the rest elected by the remaining members.[14] There are now twenty executive directors, five of whom are appointed by the five members having the largest number of shares (US, UK, Germany, France, Japan) and the rest are elected by the others.[15] The Board of Governors has the right to increase the total number of executive directors by increasing the number of those to be elected. In the thirty-five years of the IBRD's life, during which time its membership increased from 45 (in 1947) to 141 (in 1982), the number of executive directors has increased by eight.

The meeting of the executive directors, which is held in continuous session at the principal office of the Bank as required by the Articles, brings the directors in continuous contact with the management of the Bank. They normally take action upon recommendations by the management and do not concern themselves with matters of daily routine. For example, the power to approve a loan is based on the recommendation of the president, who acts on the proposals of a loan committee of the Bank staff designated by him. Similarly, the power of the executive directors to appoint the president, which, organizationally speaking, is their most important power, is based on the recommendation (nomination) of the United States, the largest stockholder.

The power of the executive directors must not be seen as separate from that of the management, and especially the president of the Bank, who acts as their chairman. During the continuous session chaired by the president, general formal transaction of Bank business takes place, mostly involving giving approval to the president's recommendations. Informal discussions are also held regularly on matters not requiring immediate formal action. It is significant to note that transcripts of informal discussions are kept secret, which indicates that more open and candid exchanges of views take place at informal sessions. It can be safely assumed that this is not limited to candor for its own sake, but that presentation of official views on current or future policies of the Bank takes place.

From the management's point of view, informal meetings held on a regular basis provide opportunities to present tentative discussions, to inform the executive directors, and to sound out their views on such matters as the state of loan applications and the result of field missions.

This continuous contact, at formal and informal levels, constitutes the principal decision-making process. In this way, the relationship between the President of the Bank and the executive directors is defined and redefined continuously. But in essence, the president proposes and the executive directors invariably accept. The process starts with the loan application. From that point up to the presentation to the executive directors of a full-fledged loan project, volumes of intricate studies and analyses are made, reports written and negotiations arranged and conducted by the Bank staff. At all levels, decision is involved: decision on technical as well as on policy matters. The president presides over the whole process, sitting at the pinnacle of corporate power.

THE PRESIDENT AND HIS STAFF

The preeminent position of the executive in the workings of an institution is a patent reality of corporate life. This is as true in business as it is in government. However, the standards of evaluation of performance are different; whereas a business executive is judged by his ability to maximize profit, in government the criteria may be as diverse as the constituencies and the requirements more complex. The World Bank, from the standpoint of institutional analysis, has a unique place in corporate experience as it belongs to neither category of government or business, nor does it fit into the post-war phenomena of supra-national institutions of the United Nations, although it is called a UN specialized agency.

The functioning of the Bank and the development of its policy, its rules, and its practices, all represent an interesting mixture of these components. Its basic thrust, however, has been "business-like." The origin of this business approach goes back to the structure of the Bank, as reflected in its reduced interest for social services. This demand was a precursor of the creation of the IDA. Pakistan asserted that trade, not aid, was needed and urged the Bank to play an increasing role in carrying out necessary policies.

By the time George Woods took over from Black in 1963, the North-South alignment was well underway. Third World membership of the Bank had increased dramatically, and with the changing political climate in the international community, with Europe's colonial empire shrinking, views on the expanded role of the Bank were firmly expressed. Woods himself reflected this view at the UNCTAD I meeting in Geneva. He said: "If the Bank is to go on being a dynamic agent of economic progress, it must adapt itself to the changing development environment and respond to the changing needs of its membership. The Bank, no less than its members, must continue to grow."

charter, and the requirements of the financial sources, notably the money markets of the United States. Its evolution has been shaped principally by those requirements, tempered by the personality and philosophy of its presidents and the demands of the times.

Through his chairmanship of the board of executive directors, the president controls the substance of the issues to be discussed by the directors, as well as the proceedings of the meetings. In addition to his formal power to call meetings, to designate chairmen of committees and subcommittees, and to announce the sense of a meeting to the executive directors, he also enjoys informal contacts with the directors. These take place through regular individual contacts and smaller group meetings involving the president, his top managerial aides, and the executive directors. All have an interest in an individual or small group approach. When matters related to the countries of their representation require closer attention, the executive directors usually deal with them outside the formal structure in a more cordial and relaxed atmosphere.

If such a "club atmosphere" can induce certain positive changes from time to time, it can also operate to impart the Bank's prevailing ideology. While personal contacts may help attenuate some of the rigors of the Charter's strictures, this happens in the context of an organizational culture which reflects a US corporate managerial style of tight control at the top. This bureaucratic/managerial imperative overrides other considerations.[16]

Over the years since the Bank came into existence as the IBRD, we see the evolution of its role, first as a bridge between "war and peace," in the words of its second president, then as an agency venturing more boldly into development schemes and technical assistance. In all this, the central role played by its president as the chief organizer and articulator of its policy is undisputed. Two presidents in particular stand out in the Bank's thirty-eight years: Eugene Black (1949-1963) and Robert McNamara

(1968-1981), both in the length of their tenure and in their impact on the Bank's role.

Eugene Black continued his predecessor John J. McCloy's policy in which the Bank's role was conceived as a "business" enterprise of global order, taking over major tasks of development from national governments as the principal source for international financing. He made certain that the Bank staff was made up of people nurtured by private enterprise. Key personnel were recruited from financial circles in New York and Europe. Black's long tenure met, at times, some challenges from Third World Bank members on the Bank's lending policy. India, for example, questioned the restriction of Bank lending to cover the foreign exchange cost of goods. Mexico demanded expansion of technical assistance for the preparation of the projects to be financed by the Bank, and asked for long-term credits at

In consequence of such reappraisal of the Bank's role, and with the start of IDA's operation, credits were provided for agriculture and education. Technical assistance and training activities received increased attention. IDA's creation and the advent of IDA funds from the governments of the industrialized countries, principally the United States, introduced an official (governmental) element into the Bank's financial sources. This reinforced the potential control of Bank policy by governments of the North, but there was clearly a mutuality of interest between governments of North and South.

McNamara's presidency was responsible for the expansion of IDA operations, in volume as well as in sectoral distribution. IDA's creation must be seen as linked to the fortune of the IBRD and, due to the need of IDA's replenishment from government sources, a more influential and persuasive president was imperative. McNamara acquitted himself in this respect. While the need for IDA replenishment enhanced the role of the executive directors, particularly of those from major donor governments, at the same time, the Bank emerged, under McNamara, with a clearer image as an institution that could mediate between the demands of the South (which by 1975 had assumed ominous aspects) and the terms and conditions maintained by the North on a number of trade, aid, and development issues. One expression of the mediating role advanced by McNamara was the proposal of an annual World Development Report. These have been appearing since 1979. The formulation of policy and the provision of technical resources by the Bank management and staff, is regarded as a significant contribution to a mediating role—as is the volume of Bank loans. To that end, the composition and size of the staff and the organizational structure is of great interest. The president has statutory power to shape this organizational structure and to determine the size and distribution of the staff.[17]

The term staff, as used here, includes both the management elite—the principal aides of the president—and the other professional staff of the Bank. The articles of agreement provide for a president and "such other officers and staff to perform such duties as the Bank may determine."[18] The president is responsible for their appointment and dismissal, subject to the general control of the executive directors who normally do not interfere in this matter.

The staff of the Bank increased slowly during the 1950s, rising from 430 in 1951 to 646 in 1960. By 1971 the total staff exceeded 2,500, reaching 4,100 five years later, and 6,300 in 1981. McNamara's presidency was responsible for a sharp increase in the staff—perhaps his greatest impact on the Bank. In 1971, three years after he took office, the professional staff was 75 percent greater than in 1968; and in 1981, the year of his retirement, it was 189 percent greater. There has been no significant increase since McNamara's retirement.[19]

Organizationally, McNamara's management style also has left its imprint. In 1973 he reorganized the Bank, establishing five regional offices at the Bank's headquarters: (1) Eastern Africa; (2) Western Africa; (3) Europe, Middle East, and North Africa; (4) Asia; and (5) Latin America and the Caribbean. Later, Asia was divided into two regions.

Each regional office is headed by a vice-president and has under its direct control most of the experts required to carry out its assigned responsibilities. Each regional office is responsible for planning and supervising tasks within its assigned countries. The regional offices contain two types of departments. Country program departments organize lending programs for the countries under their jurisdiction. Projects departments are responsible for the identification, appraisal, and supervision of specific projects in their assigned countries. They have at their disposal sector specialists on agriculture, education, public utilities, and transportation. The Bank's missions, stationed abroad in some Third World countries, report to the regional offices responsible for their area of operation.

Provision was made for a broad range of policy and operational support to the regional offices, to augment policy formulation and "quality control" capabilities. This support is provided by the Central Projects staff, to which are assigned specialists in such fields as industry, telecommunications, population and nutrition, rural development, tourism, and urbanization. The central projects staff, headed by a vice president, provides operational support primarily to the regional projects departments.

There is, of course, in this consummate network of organizational control, a loan committee which has a statutory basis.[20] Consisting of the senior vice president for operations, the vice president for finance, the vice president and general counsel, the vice president for projects staff, and the regional vice president responsible for the loan being considered, this committee is considered as the ultimate assurance of "quality and consistency" in the Bank's work. It is the responsibility of the loan committee to ensure that each loan is "financially sound, and has been prepared in accordance with the Bank's policies and procedures."[21]

Another point of note, reflecting the expansive and evolving nature of the Bank's work, is that a new vice president was appointed in 1973 to direct the activities of the personnel and administrative departments together with the organizational planning department. Additionally, a director was appointed to head external relations—to deal with information, public affairs, and international organizations. The director's rank has since been elevated to that of a vice president.

Is this expansion needed to meet the objective of the Bank as originally conceived: the optimum development of the productive resources in the borrowing countries that ultimately have to bear the cost of the expansion? Or is it a development obeying the "laws" of the bureaucratic imperative— a Parkinsonian proliferation? And what of the composition and geographic representation of the Bank staff? What, in particular, has been the proportion and input of the Third World members of the Bank? These questions are as relevant today as ever, and they are closely linked with the question of the Bank's responsibility in light of its statutory objectives.

Any vested power carries responsibilities with it and there are various facets of power implicit in an institution as complex as the World Bank. The powers of the Bank's president, as the driving force of its operations and the prime mover and shaper of its policies, are clearly demonstrated in the impressive record of Robert McNamara and by various activities of the Bank under his tenure. The president stands at the center of the institution and between its bureaucratic and financial power on the one hand, and the supposed beneficiaries of its loans—the borrowing countries—on the other.

Accountability, a democratic concept, has many aspects. In legal terms, it means responsibility to account for acts or omissions to someone independent of the powerholder. In the case of the Bank, the president's legal responsibility is to the Board of Governors. He discharges it annually at the meeting of the Board, but, as was noted earlier, this is essentially a mere formality. And the board of executive directors, the delegates of the Board of Governors, are institutionally linked with the president, who presides over their meetings and carries out the functions of his office in continuous contact with them collectively and as individuals and groups. The meetings of the board of executive directors, at which all major decisions are taken, in effect register the stamp of legality on decisions already made at the bureaucratic level. Once such approvals are given by the executive directors, they are, as much as the president, legally responsible for the decision. Individual executive directors can of course cast a negative vote on any decision or can abstain. Once again, parallels with US corporations are evident.

Clearly, however, we have to go beyond legality in this enquiry into accountability. We have first to look internally at the Bank's bureaucratic makeup, and second at the capital structure and the dominant personnel who reflect the dominant stockholders of the Bank—particularly the United States. The president of the Bank has always been a US citizen, as have many of the vice presidents and the directors of important Bank divisions. The president is of course required to discharge his duties, as are all the staff, in the interest of the international community.

To begin with, the decision to make English the working language of the Bank is a factor which reinforced the Anglo-American bias in recruitment practice, especially in the formative years. The combined Anglo-American professional staff was more than 70 percent of the total professional staff up to 1951, and more than 50 percent up to 1966—in both instances reflecting an excess of their combined proportion of total capital subscriptions. In the twenty years between 1951 and 1971, the statistics of staffing increases reflect an obvious resistance by the US-UK group to internationalization of the staff. The percentage of US-UK staff to the total was 71 in 1951, decreasing to 66 in 1960, and 42 in 1971.[22] Of more significance than their number is the Anglo-American control of key positions. As of 1987 nine vice presidents were US or UK citizens, and more than half of the principal officers, directors, and division chiefs were from the US and the UK. The President's Council, the principal advisory body on the affairs of the Bank, has been predominately a US-UK-Dutch group. US citizens alone have accounted for 40 percent or more of the Council's membership, and have played a greater role in establishing the Bank's policies and managerial style than is reflected by their number.

An apparently superfluous provision in staff recruitment is the requirement of allegiance to the Bank. This was presumably addressed to the dominant members of the Bank, since the active role of the Third World was not even entertained at the inception of the institution. The contemporary import of that injunction would have been to increase recruitment from the Third World to offset the undue influence of the dominant members. Minimal progress in this regard, even under McNamara's vaunted internationalization, must be regarded as one of the Bank's major failures. It is a sensitive topic on which criticisms abound. The articles of agreement require the president to "pay due regard to the importance of recruiting personnel on as wide a geographical basis as possible."[23] There is also a requirement for "standards of efficiency and technical competence," a requirement that may be advanced to explain the minimum progress in internationalization. A corollary argument is that trained personnel are more needed in their own countries. This belies the harsh reality of the brain drain, which goes on all the time, from the South to the North.

An equitable representation of the Third World in the Bank is a political issue linked to the demand to reshape an unfair international economic order. A fairer representation in crucial decision-making centers in international institutions is an important aspect of that demand. Such representation must go beyond a token gesture; conceivably, a fair representation might help enhance the Bank's evolving mediating role, as noted above. It may be unrealistic today to demand that the president of the Bank be from the Third World, but many of the key positions must be shared. For the personnel to be truly internationalized, the top position in that department must be held by a Third World person.

It is also imperative to make concerted efforts to insure that the Bank staff, whatever their geographic origin, live by the internationalist injunction in deed—not merely in words. The staff of the Bank who come from the Third World have a special obligation to play leading roles in such concerted efforts. This obligation assumes a moral commitment to progress in this as in other questions. It also assumes an intellectual stature that can stand up to the intimidating power inherent in an institution of the Bank's magnitude. It requires resilience and creativity in the realm of ideas about development. In short, an increase in Third World staff must be made a priority of Bank policy, and it must be accompanied by selective appointments to key positions.

To return to the question of whether the organizational expansion of the Bank has been warranted, there are at least two ways of looking at this. First, the size of any institution is linked to the extent of its activity. One subsidiary question is, therefore: are Bank personnel actively engaged? All indications are that they are; there does not seem to be, on the evidence of cursory observation, an idleness in the Bank. Quantitatively, the size of the Bank staff as a ratio to the volume of its work is not at issue. This is measurable and therefore easy to assess. Qualitatively, measurements are more problematic and subject to dispute, particularly in terms of the effect of the Bank's activities in the borrowing countries. Any failure of any particular development scheme financed by the Bank is not necessarily a test of its performance, for there are, all too often, domestic factors which may cause or contribute to such failure. Assessment of Bank performance must therefore take such factors into consideration, but the Bank cannot escape a part of the blame for failures, given its influence and levereage. The more the Bank is involved in a wide variety of sectors, the greater will be the share of its blame.

The Bank has a reputation for having at its disposal some of the most qualified people in all fields of knowledge, and for conducting its work with efficiency and vigor. An aura of "the best and the brightest" suffuses the Bank atmosphere, together with, in some cases, an arrogance which seems implicit in technical expertise. This is especially true with respect to project staff. Loan officers, belonging to the program departments, tend to be more broad-minded and sensitive to Third World view or perceptions.

Bureaucratic feuds, involving inter-departmental as well as personal differences, are resolved at the level of the division chief. Where policy questions of great significance are involved, it may take the intervention of directors or even vice presidents to resolve them. Meetings are held continually, to thrash out such policy questions. It is important to stress the limits or constraints on the president (and by extension those of the vice presidents) who can only lay down general policies while exercising high-level supervision. They thus depend on the staff at every level to carry out the policy of the Bank. Given the scope and complexity of the Bank's activity, the role of the Bank staff in the decision-making process cannot be overstressed. In this respect, the concept of decision-making cannot be limited to the final act of choice made between alternatives that have been analyzed and articulated by the staff. It must, of necessity, include the principal activities which contribute to the final choice.

CONCLUSION

The record of the World Bank in four decades of lending and technical assistance is a mixed one. The volume as well as sectoral and geographical distribution of its lending activities has been impressive, reaching an average of ten billion dollars a year in funding commitments in the 1960s, covering all regions of the Third World and a variety of sectors. The evolution of the Bank's lending policies and the growth of its organizational structure, in size and sophistication, also reflects its increased role and enhanced power and influence. This increased role and influence, enabled it to define the parameters and direction of development in many developing countries.

In terms of notable achievements, the Bank has excelled in infrastructure—hydropower, transport and communication, etc. Infrastructure is traditionally a "safe" sector for lending, with guaranteed financial returns. It has also tended to reinforce the process of resource extraction began in colonial times, principally to feed an export-oriented and urban-based development strategy. The Bank's record has also been noteworthy in the area of manpower development principally centered in the education sector. There, too, the Bank was not able to break the urban-rural dichotomy, and has been a follower of trends rather than an innovator. In fairness, it should be pointed out that the Bank could not do what any given Third World country was not able or willing to do, in this as in any other sector.

The more problematic areas lie in agriculture and industry, in which the Bank has had to grapple with contradictory policies, some derived from its own philosophy, and others stemming from those of its borrowing countries. In this respect, it is worth reiterating that the Bank's role must be analyzed in the context of an international economic and legal system in which it cannot act, for the most part, as "an honest broker," given its central position in that system. Given that position, the lending policies of the Bank have tended to reflect the ideology and interests of the dominant forces of the global system. Consequently, the benefits of its lending have not always accrued to the supposed beneficiaries—the great mass of the people of the Third World. Indeed, much of the benefits have accrued to the industrialized countries in the form of the purchase of goods and services, with some benefits trickling down to the developing countries. And the trickle down benefits have tended to be concentrated in the hands of urban or other local elites.

Clearly, the blame should not be attributed to the Bank alone, but should be shared, as noted above, by the governments of the developing countries. But again, both have been trapped by the logic of the global system which has not, indeed cannot, as things stand, address the disparities in income levels within and between countries. Even the agricultural and rural development policies began under Robert McNamara, designed to benefit the poorer section of the peoples of the developing countries—the so called New Styles Strategies—did not yield the expected results. There was no appreciable increase in food production, in the disposable income of the poor, or in the investable and marketable surpluses.

Nor was there much gain in foreign exchange, despite the emphasis laid on the cultivation of cash crops for the export market. On the contrary, there has been stagnation (and in several instances, deficit) in food production with consequent loss of foreign exchange earnings for food imports, and a deterioration in the balance of payments. The shortage in food production has been accompanied by widespread hunger in many countries of Africa, particularly in recent years, while the trade imbalance and foreign exchange crisis has resulted in low capacity utilization in industry.

As in the industrial sector, the strategy of import-substitution adopted by many Third World countries was not favored by the Bank, in most instances. The theory of comparative advantage was advanced by the Bank and by bilateral donor agencies in support of arguments against such strategy. This "economic rationality" notwithstanding, import-substitution industries flourished in most developing countries, with the Bank contributing at times in financial and technical assistance. In cases where industrial progress was made in the manufacture of processed and semiprocessed goods for export (textiles, footwear, etc.) such as in South Korea, Taiwan and the Philippines, the Bank has tended to be supportive, again on the grounds of comparative advantage. Cheaper labor costs and favourable market conditions in the industrialized world, including low tariff walls, facilitated the growth of such industries. But even in these cases, a change in the market conditions would hurt these industries.

The impact of the set of crises noted above, has been to throw the export-oriented and urban biased development strategy in turmoil. The accumulation of huge debts has simply consumed a large percentage of the foreign exchange earnings of many developing countries, exposing the fallacy of the export-oriented strategy, to which the Bank seems to be wedded. That strategy assumes, for its success, certain favorable conditions, notably the steady growth of the economy of the borrowing countries, and a constantly favorable world market for their export commodities. In the context of stagnation, or even falling productivity and uncertainties in the world commodity market, a policy of more of the same, would be a prescription for continued indebtedness and deepened dependence.

The Bank's policy of structural adjustment loans reinforces the export-oriented strategy. At the same time, the Bank has also sought to scale down the role of the public sector in the developing countries, advancing privatization as a cure to what ails some sectors of their economies. But even the Bank recognizes the limits to privatization. A.W. Clausen has said, for example:

> ... the contribution that the private sector can make to development is still little understood, and the potential too little harnessed. But let me be clear on one fundamental point. Vital as the role of the private sector may be, private enterprise cannot alone set the developing countries back on the path to sustained economic growth and social progress. How effectively governments perform in the overall management of their economies is the truly critical factor.

As a part of an effort to promote the participation of the private enterprise sector, the Bank has also advanced the concept of cofinancing. Cofinancing operations were begun by the Bank in the 1950s by associating other lending agencies with its lending programs in specific projects. The number of cofinanced projects rose in the 1970s, reaching an average of eighty projects a year in the early 1980s and totalling six billion dollars a year. The principal aim of the Bank's promotion of cofinancing is to involve private sources, especially commercial banks.

Finally, it should be noted that the World Bank, as a multilateral lending agency, is regarded by many as an institution that can mediate between the industrialized world and the developing countries, in their hitherto unresolved global contention over a number of issues. For over a decade now, the two sides have been deadlocked in the nondialogue of what has been called the North-South Dialogue. The deadlock reflects substantial differences between the approaches of the two sides on issues of trade, development aid, debt moratorium, and related issues.

In this respect, an eminent Third World economist, and at one time a senior management aide in the Bank, has contended that change in international structures is inevitable, whethere there is dialogue or not. The significance of dialogue, if it could be organized meaningfully, the contention goes, would be to help accelerate the change through common consent, and to ease the pain of transition through orderly negotiation from which "all sides gain, though not in equal measure."

The World Bank itself, under McNamara's presidency, seemed to share this perspective. Indeed, McNamara initiated the establishment of the Brandt Commission, partly in an effort to bring the "dialogue" to a meaningful stage. But that Commission was not able to sustain the momentum and practically disappeared, following the publication of the Report.[8] The Bank suffers from an indentity crisis which has inhibited its potential for a mediating role. The Bank is first and preeminently a financial institution preoccupied with financial returns, credit worthiness and the mood of the money markets. At the same time, it is also a development lending agency mandated by its charter to help develop the productive resources of its member countries. The first of its defining attributes impels it to ignore the plight and pleas of the poor, as long as the returns keep coming despite other consequences. In this, it is one with the IMF. The second attribute involves it in periodic fits of agonizing over the "poorest of the poor," "growth with equity," and so forth. Hence, McNamara's vaunted "New Styles" policy.

In the final analysis, everything boils down to the need for restructuring and powersharing in the governance of the Bretton Woods institution, if the deadlock is to be resolved and the wrongs suffered by the developing countries are to be redressed. Such a restructuring would guarantee an adequate representation of the perceptions and interests of these countries and a proper appreciation of their aspirations and interests. And it would better guarantee social and economic progress and global peace. But a restructuring is not likely in the short run, and "in the long run, we are all dead," as Keynes acidly noted.

NOTES

1. See for example, Teresa Hayter, *Aid As Imperialism*, Harmondsworth: Penguin, 1971 and Weldon Bello, et al., *Development Debacle*, San Francisco: Institute for Food and Development, 1982.
2. Cf. Edward Mason and Robert E. Asher, *The World Bank Since Bretonwoods*, Washington, D.C.: Brookings Institution, 1973. See also, Escott Reid, *Strengthening the World Bank*, Chicago: Stevenson Institute of International Affairs, 1973 and Bettina Hurni, *The Lending Policy of the World Bank in the 1970s: Analysis and Evaluation*, Boulder, Co.: Westview Press, 1980.
3. See for example, Robert L. Ayers, "Breaking the Bank", *Foreign Policy*, Summer 1981, No. 43, pp. 104-120.
4. See Chapter 3 of the present volume, especially the section on economic self-determination.
5. IMF Articles of Agreement, Art. I.
6. IBRD Articles of Agreement, Art. I.
7. See the Club of Rome, *Reshaping the International Order: A Report to the Club of Rome*, Jan Tinbergen, coordinator and Anthony J. Dolman, editor, New York: Dutton, 1976.
8. IBRD Articles of Agreement, Art. V, Sect. 2(b) and Art. II, Sect. 1(a).
9. Ibid., Art. II, Sect. 2(a).
10. Ibid., Art. V, Sect. 3(a).
11. Ibid.
12. IBRD Articles of Agreement, Art. V, Sect. 2(b).
13. These remarks and much of what follows are derived from the author's observations as a former employee of the Bank.
14. IBRD Articles of Agreement, Art. V, Sect. 4(a) and (b).
15. See the Bank's Annual Report for 1987.
16. This is especially true in the case of strong presidents such as Eugene Black and Robert McNamara. Management aides, even at the level of vice president, often act as interpreters and executors of the president's will, and their subordinates follow suit. Those with a critical disposition tend to be marginalized, with rare exceptions such as Mahbub ul Haq under McNamara.
17. IBRD Articles of Agreement, Act. V, Sect. 5(b).
18. Ibid., Art. V, Sect. 1.
19. Information, especially statistics are not as easy to obtain today as it was earlier.
20. IBRD Articles of Agreement, Art. V, Sect. 7. See also Art. III, Sect. 4(iii).
21. See Bank's Annual Report for 1973.
22. On the question of Mason and Asher, op. cit.
23. IBRD, Articles of Agreement, Art. V, Sect. 5(a).

Chapter 7
The Eritrean War and Prospects for Peace in the Horn of Africa

INTRODUCTION

The principal cause of the war in Eritrea and the instability in the Horn of Africa has been, and remains, the denial to a people of their right to self-determination, aggravated by the intervention of foreign powers. This intervention has taken ominous forms in recent years, in the scale and intensity of foreign armed involvement. At the same time the world community has been remiss in failing to bring about a peaceful resolution to this tragic conflict.

Anyone concerned about the peace, welfare and progress of the people of the area cannot ignore the historic injustice perpetrated on the Eritrean people, who have been twice wronged in modern times. The first occasion was in 1950, when a US-sponsored Resolution of the United Nations imposed federal union of Eritrea with Ethiopia. The second was in 1962, when Emperor Haile Selassie unilaterally abrogated that same federation with the tacit complicity of the whole world, leaving the Eritrean people no recourse but war.

If, as the United States claimed in 1950, "considerations of security and world peace" were the criteria by which the Eritrean people were denied their right, surely the present generation of US policymakers should acknowledge the failure of that unfortunate decision and rectify it. Such acknowledgement and rectification become the more compelling given the magnitude of the resulting tragedy of this, Africa's longest war, in which both superpowers have alternated as Ethiopia's supporters and suppliers of arms. The reversal of alliances in which the Soviet Union switched sides in 1977 has ironically left the Eritrean people worse off, pitting them against an Ethiopian regime, more powerfully backed than it was as an American ally. The Soviet alliance has introduced arms to the region on a massive scale, increasing the military power of Ethiopia tenfold from 30,000 under Emperor Haile Selassie, to over 300,000 regular troops and militia, making it sub-Saharan Africa's largest army, second only to that of South Africa.[1] This massive arms infusion, and the consequent militarization of Ethiopian society, has aggravated the instability of the region. It has also critically contributed to the famine of recent years.

What follows is a summary of the claims of the two sides—Ethiopian and Eritrean—with a brief historical analysis and discussion of the legal basis of the Eritrean case. Then a review of some of the steps taken or contemplated towards a peaceful settlement will be made, followed by some concluding remarks.

CONFLICTING CLAIMS AND PROSPECTS FOR PEACE

There have been two basic perceptions and perspectives on the Eritrean question corresponding to the two sides in the war. The Ethiopian perspective is that it confronts a secessionist rebellion whose success will not only affect Ethiopia's territorial integrity, but would have far-reaching implications for Ethiopia and the rest of the African Continent. A corollary argument holds that this "secessionist" rebellion in a sensitive area of the world has invited foreign intervention, thus disturbing the stable equation constructed in the post-colonial era by the founding fathers of the OAU. OAU principles of the territorial integrity of the post-colonial African States are thus invoked in favor of the Ethiopian side as well as the principle of non-interference in the internal affairs of a sovereign member state.

Ethiopian diplomacy from the time of Emperor Haile Selassie (one of the "founding fathers" of the OAU) to the present has assiduously and consistently advanced this *status quo* argument. The Pandora's box implications for the rest of Africa play on sensitive African nerves against a background of the tragic experiences of Katanga and Biafra. To people unfamiliar with the historical and legal bases of the Eritrean cause in particular, these implications often reduce any discussion to such emotional levels that Eritreans have had difficulty making progress in African diplomacy, until recently.

The Eritrean side bases its argument, as noted previously, on historical and legal grounds which Ethiopian diplomacy has successfully managed to cover up or misrepresent. The persistence of the Eritrean peoples' struggle and the duration of the war against formidable odds alone testify to the seriousness and validity of the Eritrean case. Indeed the Eritrean saga is an extraordinary one by any historical standards, and keeping it covered up or isolated has been a major concern of Ethiopian diplomacy. But the struggle can no longer be isolated or covered up. It has joined the mainstream of world history, even though it is wrongly characterized as a secession, primarily to deprive the Eritrean people of African support.

Why is the Eritrean struggle not a secession, and what would a change in perception imply for the future settlement of the conflict? As has been explained in more detail in previous chapters, the historical argument put forward by the Eritrean side is based on universal principles of international law and on the post-colonial applications of those principles in the African context. While it is true that respect for the sovereignty and territorial integrity of a state is a fundamental principle of international law, the Eritrean side argues that: (1) the foundation of that principle, the right to colonial peoples to self-determination and independence, was violated in the Eritrean case, and (2) the Ethiopian violations of the integrity of the colonially-determined Eritrean territory and the unilateral abrogation of the 1952 federation entitles the Eritrean people to wage a colonial war of independence.

The legal framework in which this argument is based is not even at issue. The charter of the United Nations,[2] and Several Resolutions of the UN General Assembly[3] provide this framework. What is in dispute are the specific conditions and manner in which these are invoked or sought to be applied. If the present armed conflict results in a stalemate, or if there is an Eritrean victory, the possibility of negotiations can not be ruled out. The financial and economic drain, to say nothing of the human suffering, may indeed dictate such a course of action. In that event, legal principles would assume greater significance than they have in the past. This is so because once the Eritrean case is seen as one of unfinished decolonization, and not as one of secession, pressure would be brought to bear on the parties to the dispute, to concentrate on future structures of cooperation. An honest reappraisal, in light of history and present realities, is therefore necessary.

Skeptics may dismiss this as utopian, asserting that it is military might and not legal principles that matter. Such skepticism is certainly borne out by history. The warning of the chief Czechoslovak delegate,[4] which passed unheeded, read together with the words of John Foster Dulles[5] and seen in the context of modern Eritrean history, attest that Might is Right. The law tend to favor the *status quo*, until a given state is so shaken that it is no longer considered tenable, and support begins to shift in favor of those who challenge it. In the case under discussion, the *status quo* was represented by a major African figure of international repute, who made good use of his fame. Emperor Haile Selassie lost no time in attempting to remove the basis of legitimacy on which the Eritrean case was historically grounded, in terms of the emerging post-colonial order. His timing of the illegal annexation of Eritrea was shrewd. November 1962 was only six months before the Eritrean people themselves, faced with a *fait accompli* of an imposed federation and deprived of all arms to resist, tried to make the most of their limited autonomy. But when that was taken away from them they took up arms, reclaiming their right afresh. Their story, and the story of every rebellion, is an eloquent testimony to the limits of Might. It is in recognition of its limits that Might pays tribute to Right in different forms. Resort to negotiations is one expression of such recognition.

But any established order and the prevailing principles of international founding conference of the OAU, scheduled to be held in Addis Ababa in May 1963, with the Emperor as host. The fact that he was host added procedural muscle to the prestige that he enjoyed as an elder African statesman. He succeeded in excluding any mention of the Eritrean questions from the agenda, presenting his accomodating African brethren a *fait accompli* of an annexed Eritrea, at a time when the Eritrean Liberation Front (ELF) was mounting serious offensives against his military outposts.

Then at the second OAU summit in Cairo in 1964, the colonial boundaries were accepted to define African statehood. To Eritreans, who had entertained any hope for an international intervention on their behalf, the denial of access to the OAU and the UN made amply clear that there was no alternative but to wage war until they could be strong enough to force the issue on the international community, especially the OAU. That point has now been reached after over a quarter century of war. What are the historical roots of the Eritrean case which have enabled the Eritreans to survive for so long against such heavy odds?

THE ERITREAN STRUGGLE IN HISTORICAL PERSPECTIVE

A brief historical account will help to put the Eritrean question in a different perspective from other so-called secessionist movements. Eritrea was an Italian colony between 1889 and 1941. Italian colonial rule, like other colonial rules, in African history defined a territorial entity and produced a social formation embracing a people with a sense of common national destiny. This sense of common destiny forged under a common history of oppression developed to a full-fledged movement for independence after the end of World War II. In fact, the Eritrean independence movement was one of the earliest in Africa in the post-World War II period.

As already noted, following the defeat of Italian forces in Africa, Italian colonial rule was replaced by British rule in in 1941. Then the Four Allied Powers of World War II (USA, USSR, Britain and France) signed a peace treaty with Italy under which Italy renounced her claims to her former colonies (Eritrea, Libya and Somalia), and the Four Powers would seek to dispose of the former colonies by agreement, failing which they would sumit the matter to the General Assembly of the United Nations. The Four Powers failed to agree and submitted the matter to the United Nations, which settled the future of Libya and Somalia in its Third Session (1948), but referred the Eritrean case to the Fourth Session. The Fourth Session (1949) resolved to send a Commission of Enquiry to visit Eritrea to sound out Eritrean opinion. This five-man commission presented a divided report with a minority of two (Pakistan and Guatemala) strongly advocating independence for Eritrea, and a majority (South Africa, Norway and Burma) proposing different forms of association with Ethiopia.

Following the Report of the Commission, the Fifth Session of the United Nations General Assembly (1950), with US-British stewardship, passed a Resolution (390 A(v)) under which Eritrea would be joined with Ethiopia in a federation "under the sovereignty of the Ethiopian crown," with regional autonomy for Eritrea. This federal arrangement had no built-in guarantee to protect Eritrean autonomy, which meant that in the event of Ethiopian violation of the terms of the settlement, the United Nations would have the ultimate responsibility to guarantee against any violation, or to provide remedies for any violations. Such was the view of the legal panel that drafted the Final Report.

Despite its denial of the rights of the Eritrean people, the federation recognized the national identity of the Eritrean people and their territorial integrity; provided for an autonomous Eritrean government; provided for the respect of the institutions, traditions, religions and languages of the Eritrean people. It also promised all persons in Eritrea the enjoyment of human rights and fundamental freedoms through the provision of a Bill of Rights. Moreover, it enshrined the democratic principle in Article 16 of the Eritrean Constitution (derived from Resolution 390 A(v)), which was not to be amended under any circumstances.

It is worth reiterating that the recently-released official documents of the US Government confirm the claims of Eritreans and their supporters that: (1) the majority of the Eritrean people were in favor of independence; (2) the US Government was aware of this fact; (3) the US Government had decided to support Emperor Haile Selassie's territorial claim over Eritrea, in return for his promise to be a loyal ally and to grant the United States naval, air and communications facilities in Eritrea; and (4) at the time when the UN Commission of Enquiry was sent to Eritrea, US policymakers were already charting a strategy to gain a foothold over the area with Eritrea as the critical center.[6]

Very soon after the federation came into effect in September 1952, the Emperor's Government began to undermine the whole arrangement. Violations of the terms of the federal Act took place at all levels, draining the federal and democratic principles of their essence and reducing Eritrean autonomy. Violations of human and democratic rights occurred provoking Eritreans to send urgent petitions and organize protest demonstrations, but to no avail. The Eritrean languages were replaced by the Ethiopian language of Amharic, both for purposes of official communication and for instruction. This left a whole generation of Eritreans educationally handicapped. Political parties and trade unions were banned, as well as all meetings.

Finally, in November 1962, the Emperor delivered the *coup de grace*, unilaterally abrogating the federation, sending his troops of occupation and declaring Eritrea a province of Ethiopia. In retrospect, and particularly in light of the above-mentioned newly-discovered evidence, it is easy to understand, if not to condone, the silence of the US Government in the face of a flagrant violation of the federal arrangement which it worked so hard to fashion. The silence of the US Government and the world community as a whole was tantamount to complicity. Eritrean protests and petitions sent to the United Nations fell on deaf ears.

As we reflect on the general condtions of the region and on prospects for peace, reconstruction and development, it was worth noting again that denial of fundamental human and political rights is a primary source for instability. And the denial of any recourse such as access to the UN forum to aggrieved peoples compounds the original wrong, and leads to rebellion and instability. The UN Declaration of Human Rights of 1948 envisages the consequences of such denial in its provision that such denial entitles peoples to take arms and rise in revolt.[7]

From Peaceful Protest to War of Liberation

The armed struggle in Eritrea started in precisely these circumstances. It is not sufficiently realized that the Eritrean people took up arms as a last resort, after all pleas for remedy against the Ethiopian government's violation failed to produce results. In September 1961, the transition from peaceful protest to armed struggle was proclaimed with the establishment of the Eritrean Liberation Front (ELF), which fired the first shots in the lowlands of Barka, in North-Western Eritrea. War became the final arbiter.

The ELF guerilla army grew in strength and starting inflicting serious damage on the Ethiopian security forces, by 1965. Its exploits became matters of daily discourse in town and country alike, as it galvanized public opinion. By 1968, its impact was severe enough to cause some harsh reprisals in the form of random massacres of innocent villagers, and burning and looting by the Ethiopian army. But the reprisals hardened the Eritrean will to resist and consolidated unified support for the ELF.

Meanwhile, the ELF ranks swelled with new recruits including, university and secondary school students and teachers joining from different parts of the country. The leadership of the ELF felt the pressure from the new recruits for a national democratic agenda, transcending ethnic and religious differences. The structure of the ELF organization and its patterns of command tended to reinforce regional and religious division. The tension that developed resulted in armed confrontations, recriminations, some killings and defection.

Then, in 1970, the Eritrean Peoples Liberation Front (EPLF) was formed out of splinter groups who split from the ELF. It is hardly an exaggeration to say that the history of Eritrea, and perhaps of the whole region of the Horn of Africa, has been significantly affected by the emergence and growth of the EPLF. After a few years of internecine war between the ELF and the EPLF, the EPLF eventually became the sole dominant force in Eritrea.

From its inception, out of the crisis of the ELF, the EPLF gave primacy to political education. Political and social goals of democratic transformation were clearly defined for the national liberation struggle to achieve. Beyond the military victory and the winning of national independence, a program of social transformation was envisaged, and impressed upon EPLF members, under which the general mass of the Eritrean people would be not only independent but masters of their own lives. Politics must command arms, and not vice versa, and the leadership must be democratically accountable.

These principles and precepts, applied in the daily practice of the guerilla army, and manifestly apparent to the public, together with the discipline, determination and experience of the guerilla army explain the triumph of the EPLF over the ELF, during their three-year war, and also over the Ethiopian army. Since 1975, a large number of technically qualified Eritreans joined the EPLF, and in the context of the factors noted above, transformed the guerilla army into a technically proficient, resourceful and resilient national army.

Social services in health and education were organized extensively and land reforms and technical agricultural services were attempted in the highlands, until the Soviet-backed military campaign of the Dergue interrupted them. Elected village assemblies administered their local affairs. The liberation of women from age-old double oppression ensured their full participation in the struggle, one-third of the EPLF army are women.

Since 1978, the EPLF survived eight major Soviet-backed Ethiopian offensives, each time involving not less than 80,000 troops, tanks, heavy weapons and monopoly of the skies. The EPLF withdrew from the highlands around Asmara in 1978, before the start of the offensives. The defeat of the Ethiopian army, especially in the sixth offensive in 1982, signaled not only the survival of the EPLF, but the beginning of a new strategic offensive. Its capture of heavy weapons in 1984 increased its capability to start a counter-offensive, and recapture lost ground. Since that time, the trend has been for the EPLF to continue its counter-offensive. This process culminated in the capture of Afabet and the decimation and capture of 18,000 Ethiopian troops together with three high-ranking Soviet officers. Previous Western speculation of an endless stalemate seems to have changed in favor of a prognosis of an Eritrean victory barring Soviet intervention as in Afghanistan.

WHERE DO WE GO FROM HERE?

We have outlined the historical background of the Eritrean struggle, and the legal framework under which the conflicting claims are made. The stakes are also clear. For the Eritreans, it is an independent state. For Ethiopia, it is continued occupiation, justified in terms of the need for access to the sea, and fear that an independent Eritrea might inspire secessionist aspirations of other national groups within Ethiopia proper leading to the country's disintegration.

Unfortunately, foreign interests, as was already noted, have further complicated the matter. Our analysis of the Eritrean war must therefore take these foreign interests into account. There are two paths to settlement: one is a conclusive military victory by one side, the other is a peaceful settlement, either through negotiations of the EPLF and the Ethiopian government, or a submission of the question to an internationally supervised referendum, or a combination of the two.

Leaving aside the question of military victory by one side, which may or may not be forthcoming soon, what are the prospects for a peaceful settlement? There have been some meetings between the EPLF and the Dergue over the last ten years, which were arranged quietly by third parties. In almost every case, the Dergue followed the meeting with a major military campaign against the EPLF, presumably believing that the EPLF was suing for peace, out of military weakness. This perception proved to be wrong each time, and the EPLF has now made it clear that if there are to be any future meetings, there must be a public declaration that such a meeting was being held and that the mediating party must be named publicly.[8]

The EPLF made a proposal in November 1980 for a peaceful settlement. In brief, it proposed that an internationally supervised referendum should be held under which the Eritrean people would choose between full independence, federal association with Ethiopia, or regional autonomy within Ethiopia. The Dergue did not respond to this offer.[9]

The "mediators" who quietly arranged the past meetings, such as the East Germans in 1978, have been parties that may be considered as the Dergue's allies, although some have been supporters of the Eritrean cause in the past. The hidden hand of Soviet diplomacy is partly visible in some of these endeavors. What of the OAU, the UN and Western countries?

Several half-hearted attempts have been made by past chairmen of the OAU summit, notably former presidents Siaka Stevens of Sierra Leone, and Nimeiry of Sudan. All failed, because of Ethiopian reluctance, for fear that the process would lend legitimacy to the "rebels." The late president Sekou Toure of Guinea, attempted to include the Eritrean question as an item on the OAU agenda. Again, Ethiopian diplomacy prevailed. The privileged position of Ethiopia, notably because of the fact that the OAU headquarters is in Addis Ababa, has been helpful to the Ethiopian side.[10]

The UN response to Eritrean entreaties has been to say that it is a regional question that must be handled by the regional body, i.e., the OAU. The UN has not, as yet, agreed to accept its historic responsibility to include the Eritrean question in its agenda, again because of Ethiopian diplomacy, now powerfully backed by Soviet power. This is so, as we have seen despite authoritative legal opinion declaring that the United Nations should be seized of the matter.[11]

What is the position of the powers that were responsible for the historic wrong, namely, the United States of America and Britain? Are they willing to reverse their earlier positions and support, in principle at least, the Eritrean quest for self-determination? Or, are they interested in a peaceful settlement, at the very least?

There is no evidence to suggest that US policy makers are prepared to review the mistakes and wrongs of the past, despite the reversal of alliances noted above, such is the power that Ethiopia holds in the minds of the policy-makers aided by the bureaucratic inertia which favors a continuation of the *status quo*, however unjust.[12] There is also an expectation that one day soon Ethiopia would be recovered from the "Soviet embrace," and Ethiopia is a bigger prize worth waiting for. Implicit in this expectation is an assumption that the Soviets will make blunders and be expelled from

Ethiopia as they have been from Egypt, Sudan and Somalia. Their massive military presence and single-minded drive to establish a Moscow-brand communist party in Ethiopia, which has already happened, does not apparently worry US policymakers. The poor performance of the Ethiopian economy, the unpopularity of the regime, the heavy-handed methods of the Soviets, it is hoped, will soon change the situation. These are clearly serious gambles.

The EPLF, on its part, has not been energetic in approaching the Americans, mindful of America's past performance and present behavior. The EPLF is also constrained by other considerations. The cornerstone of its strategy, both political and military, is self-reliance, which in the political field, means freedom from dependence on any foreign source of support, and the avoidance of any vulnerability. The EPLF's diplomatic work, as in all other areas, has been incremental in its development, building on sure and carefully selected bases. But in periodic appeals made to the international community, it has of course included the United States. Some Eritreans and foreign supporters have complained of the slow progress of the EPLF's appeal to the West, and in particular in not singling out the United States as the object of a sustained diplomatic initiative. In their view, the EPLF should cultivate the United States as a political supporter in principle, without compromising its strategy of self-reliance. They contend, as the Somalis do, that since the Ethiopians are "leaning on a huge (Soviet) mountain" necessities of survival dictate that the Eritreans should lean on the US. It is open to debate whether: (1) the US policymakers would respond positively to Eritrean demands, and (2) whether their support would leave the strategy of self-reliance uncompromised. And some ask whether it is necessary now.

One thing is certain, United States' interests cannot be served by continued warfare and instability in such a sensitive region. It can even be argued that local wars in areas where the interests of both superpowers are involved, as in the Middle East and the Persian Gulf, constitute a serious danger which could lead to nuclear war.[13] Certainly, American interests in the Horn of Africa, including the Sudan, in the adjoining Arabian peninsula and beyond, lie in peace. And the best guarantee for regional peace—one that will be lasting—is a framework under which the quest for justice of aggrieved peoples is satisfied, while the interests of neighboring states are also secured.

To promote peace the United States should use its enormous power to encourage the warring parties to come to the negotiation table and to insist that the Soviet Union do the same. Whether a referendum is held under international supervision, or whether there are direct negotiations between the Eritreans and the Ethiopians, it should now be clear that there cannot be regional peace unless the right of the Eritrean people to determine their political future is recognized. On the other hand, the interests of Ethiopia in an access to the sea would be a major subject of contention. Once Eritrea's independence is accepted, the legal framework for the implementation of an agreement in principle can be subject to negotiation.

As for Ethiopia's fear of disintegration, a recent statement of the EPLF on this issue should put the matter in proper perspective.[14] While the EPLF supports the principle of a democratic transformation of Ethiopia, and supports democratic movements fighting the Dergue, it does not aim to dismember Ethiopia. At the same time, it regards the "Ogaden question" in a different light, given the Ogaden's recent history in which Britain ceded it to Ethiopia in the latet 1940's, at a time when the Somalis in the area were actively demanding self-determination and the reunification of all Somalis.[15]

The positions of the British, the French and some other European parties have been undergoing drastic changes in the recent past, which is most encouraging to the Eritrean cause and for peace in the region. For example, in a preface to a book co-authored by Stewart Holland, British Labour Party Shadow Minister for Overseas Development, Neil Kinnock, the British Labour Party leader has written:

> In Eritrea, hundreds of thousands of children, women and men, have been killed or crippled, or turned into refugees in a war which began almost a quarter century ago ... In our programme ... we pledged support for self-determination for the people of Eritrea. We promised financial and material support for the Eritrean Peoples Liberation Front and the Eritrean Relief Association. We gave our backing to the proposal of the EPLF that there should be an internationally supervised referendum on the future of Eritrea—a referendum which would allow the Eritrean people to choose between full independence from Ethiopia, federal association with Ethiopia or regional autonomy within Ethiopia.[16]

This courageous initiative and principled stand may set in motion a process of reappraisal, including conceivably, by policymakers in Washington. On the whole, European socialist and social democratic parties have made similar expressions of support. For instance, the French and Italian socialist parties have made firm commitments of support. In Africa, the African section of the Socialist International under the leadership of former Senegalese President Leopold Sedar Senghor has made a similar commitment, as has Mozambique's FRELIMO.

Outside government and party circles, an increasing number of private organizations, professional and scholarly associations, religious and civic leaders, writers and other individuals have expressed their support of the right of the Eritrean people to self-determination, invariably urging a peaceful settlement. These include a growing number of young African intellectuals and student groups, some of whom express anger at the unfortunate fate of Eritrea, as well as admiration for the EPLF's achievements.

What does all this mean in terms of an early peaceful settlement of the conflict? It means, above all, that the Eritreans have broken out of the isolation to which astute Ethiopian diplomacy and resources had consigned them for over two decades. It means further that a cutting edge of interested and influential public opinion is being forged, which can eventually persuade governments, including the government of the United States, to be true to their rhetorical commitment to the principles of self-determination and the rule of law and help in the settlement of a conflict whose resolution is long overdue. It would be fitting if the OAU could take the initiative towards that worthy objective.

In conclusion, five points should be outlined: first, and foremost, the conflict in the Horn of Africa has been complicated and aggravated by the advent of Soviet power in the region, and its resolution has been indefinitely postponed by this intervention. This has altered the balance of power and hurt the cause of liberation of peoples in Eritrea and elsewhere in the area. In view of this altered reality, the liberation fronts need to clarify their strategic vision, and perhaps redefine their tactical alignments. Second, a peaceful settlement of this conflict is in the interest of all the people of the region who have suffered the horrors of war and famine. This interest coincides with that of the liberation fronts notably the EPLF, who have offered a cease-fire and a peaceful settlement. The war policy and politics of the Dergue, on the other hand, are clearly not in the interest of the Ethiopian or Eritrean peoples. Third, the Dergue and especially Mengistu, who monopolizes all decisions on Eritrea, have a stake in the continuation of the war not only because of the survival imperative of the empire, but also because of their own survival needs. They have clearly decided that they cannot survive a peaceful settlement in Eritrea, where their policy has already cost the lives of over 200,000 Ethiopian soldiers including all the best trained officers. Their rhetoric of the defense of the "Motherland" should be seen in that light, especially by Ethiopians. Furthermore, Soviet strategic interest coincides with the interest of the Dergue in that an earlier resolution would impede the transformation of Soviet military presence into a permanent political presence, which needs a longer time. There is thus a mutual dependence between the Dergue and their military backers. Hence, the adoption of a Moscow-brand communist party and a Kremlin-drafted constitution of a "Peoples Democratic Republic of Ethiopia". Fourth, the United States and its Western allies, as well as African states, can no longer be neutral observers of what is happening in Eritrea and the rest of the region. The time has come when they have to make a principled stand on the right of the Eritrean people to determine their future. The UN and the OAU should be urged to play active roles in a peaceful resolution of the war and to bring pressure to bear on the Soviet Union to that end.

Finally, the experience of the famine, and the response of the international community in helping to alleviate it, has demonstrated that an aroused public opinion, aided by an effective media campaign, and guided by the community of private voluntary agencies, can stimulate governments and the UN system to work to avoid disaster. The public response and its impact on government marks the triumph—albeit temporary—of moral principles over considerations of power politics and the bureaucratic process. More attention needs to be paid to the role of the private voluntary sector, as a humanizing force in a world dominated by power politics.

NOTES

1. It is estimated that $4½ billion worth of Soviet arms has been delivered to Ethiopia since 1977. This is roughly equal to the annual G.D.P., according to World Bank figures.
2. Articles 1 and 55.
3. Cf. Resolution 1514 and 2526.
4. The relevant passage of the Czechoslovak delegate reads: "Contrary to the fundamental purpose of the (UN) Charter it (Resolution 390 A(v/ of 1950) would deny the people of Eritrea the right of self-determination and impose on them a federation with Ethiopia which the great majority oppose. Instead of maintaining peace in that part of the world, the Resolution would foster civil discord. Instead of assisting an oppressed and exploited people to achieve freedom and independence, it would attempt to cover up the annexation of a small State by a large State . . . The Czechoslovakia delegation will never be a party to intrigues against the freedom of peoples." (Leader of the Czechoslovakia delegation to the United Nations, 1950.)
5. John Foster Dulles said: "From the point of view of justice, the opinions of the Eritrean people must receive consideration. Nevertheless, the strategic interest of the United States in the Red Sea basin and consideration of security and world peace makes it necessary that the country has to be linked to our ally Ethiopia." (John Foster Dulles, head of US delegation to the United Nations, 1950.) Quoted in Linda Heiden, "The Eritrean Struggle for Independence," Monthly Review Press, 30.2 (June, 1978):15.

6. Cf. Letter of US Secretary of Defense, James Forrestal, to Secretary of State, Dean Acheson, December 11, 1948; Department of State Memorandum of Conversation, March 30, 1949; Department of State Internal Memo issues as a guideline for the US delegation at the UN General Assembly, e.g., Secret Internal Memo of September 1948. Cf. also Incoming Telegram, August 22, 1949 from US Consul in Asmara to US Secretary of State, No. 171, August 19, 1949.
7. See the Preamble of the Declaration.
8. See EPLF statement, September 10, 1985.
9. See a 1984 Statement "The Sole Truth and the Only Way," Addis Ababa, Kuraz Press a Government Printing Press, 1985.
10. Sekou Toure openly stated that he would raise the question at the Nairobi Summit in 1981. Mengistu begged him to pass it up just that time. (Reported personally to the writer by Colin Legum.)
11. See for example, the judgement of the Permanent Peoples' Tribunal, Milan 1980; The opinion of the International Commission of Jurists, Review, and the report of the UN Commission on Eritrea.
12. Conversations and correspondence with some State Department officials indicate, however, that there is a growing sentiment among US policymakers that there should be a political solution. President Reagan gave a speech at the UN General Assembly in 1985, which expressed this sentiment.
13. Cf. Richard Nixon, Foreign Affairs, Fall 1985.
14. See "The EPLF and its Relations with the Democratic Movements in Ethiopia," February 1985. See also "The Resolutions and Final Declaration of the Second Congress of the EPLF," March 1987. Appendix - below.
15. Ibid.
16. Preface to "Never Kneel Down," by James Firebrace and Stewart Holland, Red Sea Press, 1984.

Chapter 8
Conclusion

Rather than summarize the contents of the various chapters, some of the major questions examined in them will be taken up in the context of the prevailing reality of international relations. We start this concluding chapter with the theme running through most of the essays, one which constitutes the principal problem of international relations, namely, the relationship between the theory and practice of law and politics, or rather the breakdown in such relationship.

The case of Eritrea and the role of the United Nations on Eritrea's modern, tragic history, illustrates such failure with blinding clarity. For that reason, among others, Eritrea and the United Nations was selected as the title and central focus of the present volume of essays. As was noted in previous chapters, Eritrea epitomizes the failure of international law, particularly on the subject of the self-determination of colonized peoples in the era of decolonization. The essence of the Eritrean case, like that of Namibia, is that it is a case of denied decolonization. The persistence of the Eritrean people in their quest for national self-determination, fighting alone against heavy odds, stands not only as a testimony to their tenacity and resilience, but also as a monument to the validity of the principles of equal rights and self-determination of peoples enshrined in the UN Charter.

The United Nations, which has a historic responsibility for the fate of the Eritrean people, has shirked that responsibility. In summing up the discussion on the United Nation's, international law, and self-determination as applied—or rather misapplied—to Eritrea, we must stress the lessons learned from the case of this unfortunate country. The lessons are not encouraging, but there should be no place for despair in an essay on the proper apprehension of reality.

First, the United Nations is a microcosm of the world's state system, reflecting the set of interests and attitudes of governments around the world. Governments, not peoples, are represented at the United Nations. State sovereignty is a fundamental fact of interntional relations and determines much of the character and behavior of governments. One of the consequences of this fact is the access to resources open to states, which are denied to national groups or peoples within a given state. For example, when the World Bank extends to Ethiopia financial assistance worth $300 million and the EEC another $400 million, these sums release equivalent amounts to help the Ethiopian government in the prosecution of its war in Eritrea. This is a supreme irony, underlying the state sovereignty principle.

Another application of the state sovereignty principle, again to take an Ethiopian example, concerns events during the recent famine. The Ethiopian government did not make relief aid available to the Eritrean region, the northern area being one of the worst affected. Whether the government was not able or willing to make relief available is debatable; the fact is, it did not make it available. The Eritreans have argued that food has been used as a weapon of combat, this argument borne out by the systematic air raids against civilians to disrupt ploughing, harvesting, and livestock herding. Evidently, the international relief community must have believed the Eritrean argument, for it organized cross-border operations from the Sudan—whereupon, the Ethiopian goverment protested on the grounds of interference in its internal affairs. But this time, the moral imperative prevailed over the technical arguments.*

What this experience brought into high relief was that vital resources were closed to the Eritreans as a consequence of being denied their right to become a sovereign state. It demonstrated some of the perils implicit in the sovereignty principle, if it is to be left unchecked. In their uphill diplomatic struggle, the Eritreans have found that the exclusive membership of Ethiopia in the UN club—exclusive of the Eritreans—has enabled Ethiopia to distort and misrepresent their case.

Another point to be stressed, related to the sovereignty principle, concerns the relationship between force and morality in international relations. This is an aspect of the relationship between the theory and practice of law and politics noted earlier. A proper grasp of the relationship between force

---

*Indeed, diplomats including Americans, now openly charge the Dergue with deliberate policy of starvation in the 1988 famine. See Sheila Rule, *New York Times*, April 30, 1988.

and morality is important, especially for anyone involved in the deadly struggle between contending powers in international politics, as the Eritreans have been for two generations. In this context, diplomacy becomes the art of persuading governments not only of the justice of your cause, but also of the determination with which you intend to pursue the ends of that cause, come what may.

Diplomacy, in essence, is a function of the interplay of national interest and certain commonly held, or universally recognized, principles. History teaches that, more often than not, interests prevail over other considerations. At the same time, naked power alone, based on brute force and mobilized in the service of selfish interests completely devoid of morality, results in disaster. The fall of empires throughout history has been accompanied or preceded by moral decay at the center.

Conceding then that national interest (and invariably within nations, class interest) is the primary variable explaining state behavior, we must also note the operation of moral principles. For interest alone would leave unexplained the moral and ethical aspects of the human condition: of man-in-society. All political societies are marked by a dual character, as philosophers of different times and climes have taught. There is, on the one hand, a moral side to man that enthrones reason; and, on the other hand, a "brutish" side that puts total reliance on force. The state is built out of these two aspects of human nature. The success of any state project depends on the skill with which it can weave coercion and conscience into an optimal working relationship.

The Eritrean story is an instructive case study of the interplay of these two sides of man and state. For the Eritreans, the principal lesson has been that power backed by force is a necessary condition for gaining attention and eventual recognition. Another lesson has been the growing and significant role of non-governmental organizations (NGOs) which represent active social forces in all states that are primarily driven by the moral imperative, and that can exert considerable pressure on governments. They do so in the name of the commonly held principles noted above. It was the forceful intervention of some of these NGOs that called the technical (legal) bluff of the Ethiopian government in 1985 by organizing cross-border operations. However, it must be pointed out that some governments, including the US government, backed their efforts by channeling relief aid through them. It was one of the rare moments when moral principles triumphed over brute force, although admittedly backed by some state power. The role of the NGOs should thus be looked into more closely by scholars and others alike.

Finally, we must note the larger and more complex aspects of contemporary international relations. In the introductory chapter of these essays, an attempt was made to place the development of international law and practice into a larger, historical perspective, from ancient times through the advent of the capitalist mode of production and colonial rule down to our own times. The intention was to provide a historical point of departure for the discussions that followed. In the process, some repetition was unavoidable and the discussions have raised more questionsd than they have answered.

As has been noted repeatedly in these essays, there is as yet no enforceable system of international law, unlike domestic law. This is the principal challenge of international relations. The problems facing the United Nations represent the complexity, the fascination, and the tragedy of political life, to paraphrase the late E.H. Carr. [E.H. Carr, *The Twenty Years Crisis, 1919-1939*, Harper and Row, 1945, p. 93.] But in noting the failures of the United Nations, we must also point out its record of success in several areas, particularly in the economic and social fields. Even in the political arena, taken globally, the UN has played some positive roles. One major example will suffice in this respect, one which has not found favor with what has come to be known as the North—the industrial countries of Europe, North America, and Japan.

In 1974, NIEO (the Third World demand for a new international economic order) entered the world stage with a bang, as the UN General Assembly passed a resolution giving it the stamp of legitimacy. But it was to leave the stage with a whimper. In fact, the early 1970s seemed to usher in a new era in international relations, sparked by the rise in oil prices and the consequent emergency of OPEC's power. It seemed to promise some significant changes, benefitting the Third World which had started demanding rectification of historic wrongs committed against its peoples. The North-South divide and the need for a readjustment in trade and financial relations had become the dominant themes of international discourse. NIEO registered that discourse.

Today a pervasive sense of crisis, and in some instances, of despondence, has replaced the earlier mood of optimism and the accompanying combative spirit in the Third World. There are national and global dimensions to this crisis. Nationally, governments face—and often face down—angry and hungry peoples groaning under debt burdens, who feel that they have been cheated of what was due them. Then there are global forces, beyond popular control, that have become a part of the problem, instead of the solution, as originally promised. The International Monetary Fund (IMF) is perceived as a major culprit among such global forces. IMF "conditionality" prescribes that governments must cease and desist from subsidizing food prices, for example. When governments in need of IMF loans to pay their debts follow the IMF prescription, "food riots" follow, which are in turn followed by a reversal of policy—back to food subsidy. The primary political imperative for regimes in power is to stay in power. And so, the problems continue.

The issue has now become not how much or when governments can deliver, but whether they are indeed capable of delivering the goods and services, the munificence promised on the eve of elections or successful *coup d'etats*. Moreover, national problems can no longer be analyzed in isolation, outside the global context, even when domestic policies and politics account for much of what ails Third World countries. The most obvious example of the linkage between domestic and global politics is the debt burden. "Development lending" coming out of the coffers of the World Bank and the US-AID has not helped in attacking the root causes of underdevelopment and poverty.

Even at the time when there was an increased volume of capital flow from the industrial North to the "developing" countries, the net gain accrued back to the North. As Argentina's president, Raul Alfonsin complained:

> ... We are more and more discriminated against in the placement of our traditional products... And on top of it all, we face the unbearable burden of foreign debt which—just by paying the interest—takes up a significant part of our savings capacity while traditional influx of capital from the industrialized nations has stopped. Thus, during the last five years Latin America has transferred to the developed countries more than $100 billion, dramatically decreasing our investment possibilities to restart the economic growth we desperately need. [Address to the Carter Institute of Emory University and the Institute of the Americas, Nov. 17, 1986.]

In this climate of crisis the United Nations and its specialized agencies (such as the World Bank) should play useful roles mediating conflicting claims. But the primary factors noted above which characterize the United Nations, as the organized reflection of the state system, militate against such positive roles. Egoistic national interests compete with the collective interests which should underlie true interdependence.

If history is any guide, the rectification and readjustment demanded by the Third World will not be granted out of charitable motives on the part of the industrial countries, be they from the West or the Eastern bloc. And whether the Third World can muster the requisite unity and resilience to force major concessions on the issues of fair terms of trade, aid, and a fair share in the governance of international organizations like the World Bank, time will tell.

Meanwhile, attention continues to be focused on the issues implicit in the demand for a new, and more just, world order. Conferences and seminars abound, and a number of publications have appeared touching on various aspects of the subject. Two works by two prominent Third World authors serve to illustrate this enduring interest. One is Sir Arthur Lewis' concise but pithy book on the origin and evolution of the international economic order. [Sir W. Arthur Lewis, *The Evolution of the International Economic Order*, Princeton: Princeton University Press, 1979.] The other is Mohamed Bedjaoui's *Towards a New International Economic Order* [UNESCO, Paris: Holmes & Meier, 1979.]

Professor Lewis, a Nobel Laureate in Economics, examines the origin of the division of the world into the industrial and underdeveloped countries. He contends that high agricultural productivity and a good investment climate enabled European countries to industrialize rapidly. The favorable terms of trade which they enjoyed assured them, and later North America, continued dominance over the tropical countries. One important conclusion he reaches is that market processes influenced trade patterns more than institutional forces, resulting in the flow of resources not from "rich countries" to "poor countries", as is commonly supposed, but the other way around. [See Chapters 2 and 3.]

The "developing" countries continue to depend on the markets of the industrial countries for their growth, and they continue to trade on unfavorable terms, buying dear and selling cheap. Mohamed Bedjaoui, an Algerian lawyer-statesman, now a judge in the World Court at the Hague, takes up this subject and the topic of NIEO where the UN General Assembly resolution left off. His approach is that of an international lawyer. UNESCO, in sponsoring Bedjaoui's book, expressed fervent hope that the series of which this book was the first would "exert a great deal of influence on the development of the role of international law in transforming the structures of societies." [Preface to Bedjaoui, op cit.]

A scholar-practitioner, Bedjaoui was a key figure in the Algerian government of the late president Boumedienne, who presented the proposals for NIEO to the UN General Assembly in 1974 in his capacity as chairman of the Non-Aligned Movement. The book launches the discussion under the telling title of: "International Order of Poverty and Poverty of International Order." This title admirably sums up the essence of the problem of international relations from a Third World perspective. Indeed, the book should be compulsory reading, especially in Third World universities.

If Hugo Grotius were alive today I would like to think that he would discern a future, and more just, international order, necessarily growing out of the need for mutual benefit, and hence, mutual readjustment. Such a readjustment in the end would result in true interdependence. What passes as interdependence today is, in actual fact, the continued dominance under a sophisticated guise of the powerful countries of the industrial world over a dependent Third World.

The continued denial by the powerful North of the just demands of the weak South, like the continued denial of the just demands of the Eritrean people, carry with them the risk of prolonging pain and tragedy into a future of uncertain perils. In the one case, the worst scenario is the possibility of a series of debt defaults which could spell disaster for the international financial and trading system. Everyone would be hurt by such a disaster with the North being the worst hit, as in the Depression. In the other case, the worst scenario would be an Afghanistan-type of Soviet intervention on Ethiopia's side. Given the Eritrean will and strength to resist, the outcome of such an intervention would be tantamount to genocide.

The link between the two cases should be obvious. In both instances, continued denial is based on the arrogance of power and egoistic interest. And in both cases, a return to first principles based on a community of interests is the answer. Paradoxically, a Third World which waxes eloquent at the UN on the issue of an unjust international order, is itself guilty of ignoring just demands, including the compelling demands of the Eritrean people. There should be no double standard. Justice, like peace, is indivisible. To be selective in the proper application of the principles of justice—of self-determination—is to undermine in advance the justice of your own demands.

Index

Abortive coup, 110, 111
Acheson, D., 31, 32
Adua, battle of, 104
Afabet, 150
Afghanistan, 14, 104
Aga Khan, S., 14, 104
Ahmed Buna, 121
Akehurst, M., 24
Aklilu Habte-Wold, 32, 35, 41
Alfonsin, R., 161
Algeria, war of, 8; willayas in, 48
All-African Peoples Conference, 62
Amhara, 105
Amharic, 44, 105
Amin, S., 72, 125
Andargachew Mesai, 42
Angola, intervention in, 102
Annexation, 2, 49, 50; strategy of, 51
Arabian Sea, access to, 99
Arabic, 44
Asfah Kahsai, 121
Asfaha Wodle Mikael, 44 45
Austin, J., 24
Australia, 4
Austro-Hungarian Empire, 58
Awate, Hamid Idris, 48
Axum, 103
Axumite Empire, 81

Bab-al Mandab, 112
Babu, A.M., 97

Badian, E., 21
Ball, M.G., 25
Bandung, 19; conference of, 68
Bangladesh, 68
Barka, 149
Barnet, R., 24
Bedjaoui, M., 19, 25, 162
Belgium, 64
Bentham, J., 38
Berbera, naval facilities in, 117
Berlin Treaty, 5, 61
Bevans, 22
Bevin-Sforza, attempts at partition of Eritrea, 30
Biafra, 87, 93, 144
Bill of Rights, 42, 86
Bimbi, G., 121
Bismark, 58
Black, E., 131, 132
Black Sea, Soviet shipping lanes from, 99
Bobrov, P.L., 6, 9, 13, 23, 24
Bolshevik Revolution, 5
Bonaparte, L., 58
Brandt Commission, 140
Bretton Woods System, 124
Brierly, 24, 92
Brind, H., 120
Boumedienne, H., 70
Britain (U.K.), 4, 28, 30, 33, 78
British, Act of Parliament, 8; commonwealth, 8, 63; Empire, 8, 63; manufactured goods, 4, 5
Burma, 8, 51
Bylorussia SSR, 30

Cairo, conference of, 68
Cameroun, plebiscite of, 87, 88
Canada, 4
Cao-Huy-Thuan, 56
Capitalist development, 4
Carr, E.H., 160
Carter Administration, policy on human rights and arms supply, 101, 102, 113, 117
Carter, C., 21, 22
Carthage, 3
Causus Belli, 5
Chaliand, G., 121
Chernobyl, 14
Chevron Oil Co., 121
Chile, 5

China, opium wars of, 4
Christian scribes, 103
Churchill, W.S., 23, 62
Clausen, A.W., 139
Codification, use of, 74
Cofinancing, concept of, 139
Colombo, conference of, 68
Colonial boundaries, 85, 86
Commission of Enquiry on Eritrea, 147, 148
Communaute, 8
Confederation of Ethiopian Trade Unions, 111
Conflict in the Horn, nature and sources of, 103-109
Connell, D., 121
Convention Peoples Party, 63
Coptic Church, 51
Cuba, as chair of non-aligned countries, 102
Cyrenaica, 30

D'Amato, A.A., 23
Debt, Default, scenario on, 163
Decolonization, 3, 7, 8, 19, 76, 79, 80, 81
Dienbienphou, 62
De Gaulle, C., 8
Democratic Government, principles of, 41, 43, 86
Denmark, 7
Deressa, 34
Dergue, 65, 103, 112; response to U.S. warning over Somalia, 118; accord with Libya and South Yemen, 118
Deutch, K., 89
Dillon, W., 62
Dimetros, G.M., 44, 45, 51
Diplomacy, 3, 4
Dines, M., 121
Disraeli, 60, 62
Djibouti, 82, 109
Drew, Brigadier, 34
Dulles, J.F., 37, 79, 106, 145
Dumbarton Oaks, UN Charter, version thereof, 63
Dutt, P., 22, 23

East India Company, 5
East-West relations, 102
Eckstein, H., 96
Economic self-determination, 67
European Economic Community (EEC), 158
Egypt, 48

Emerson, R., 61, 66
Empire, expansion of, 42
Engels, F., 58
Eritrean Assembly, 39, 42, 43, 52, 88; resolution concerning banning of *Voice of Eritrea* newspaper, 83
Eritrean Constitution, 38, 39, 40, 51, 85
Eritrean Flag, 84
Eritrean Independence Bloc, 34
Eritrean Labor Movement, 43; general strike of, 45, 46, 84
Eritrean Liberation Front, 7, 10, 47-49, 84, 146-149
Eritrean Liberation Movement, (Haraka), 46, 49, 84, 103
Eritrean Peoples Liberation Front, 48, 92, 93, 107, 149-152
Eritrean Liberation Struggle, 106-107
Eritrean Relief Association, 153
Erlich, H., 96
Ethiopian diplomacy, 144
Ethiopian state, 100-101, 105
Ethiopian perspective on Eritrean question, 144

Falk, R., 15, 23, 24
Famine, in the Horn region, 1972-74, 111; 1984-85, 155
Farer, T., 117, 122
Federation, 85; Federal Act, 38, 40, 43, 50, 81, 83, 85; Federal idea, 38; Federal scheme, 39
Fenet, A., 39, 56
Feudal Power, 42
Fezan, 30
Firebrace, J., 158
Florence, city state of, 4
Forrestal, J., 31, 32
Four Powers, disagreements of, 28; negotiation among, 29; Commission of investigation of, 29
Franck, T., 94
FRELIMO, 153
French Revolution, as source of nationalism, 61
Freund, B., 22
Friedman, W., 11, 23, 90

General Agreement on Tarif and Trade (GATT), 125
Germany, 3, 7
Gondar, 103
Goodrich, 25
Gram-Rudmann, Amendment of, 25
Greece, 3, 7
Greenfield, R., 52
Grenada, 102

Grotus, H., 4, 162
Guatemala, 31
Guinea, 23
Gunder Frank, A., 72, 125

Haile Selassie, 29, 32, 35, 36, 45, 49, 75; size of army of, 144
Hailey, Lord, 71
Haraka (*see also* Eritrean Liberation Movement), 46
Halliday, F., 121
Hart, H.L.A., 11, 12, 13, 24
Heiden, L., 121
Higgins, R., 94
Hodgkin, T., 61
Hoffman, 94
Holland, S., 153
Holocaust, 74
Hong Kong, cession of, 5
Human rights, 76
Hune, S., 72

Ibrahim Sultan Ali, 47
Idris Mohamed Adam, 47
Imperial order No. 27, as instrument of longstanding imperial strategy of annexation, 51, 52
India, 4, 8
Indigenous forces, autonomy of, 100
International Commission of Jurists, 82, 86, 89
International covenants, on political, social and economic rights, 78
International law, development of, 4
Iran, 102
Iraq, 30
Ireland, 64
Islamic League, 47
Israel, 99
Italy, renunciation of colonial possession, 28

Jennings, W.I., 23, 37, 38, 85
Jesus Christ, royal genealogy with, 103
Jus Gentium, 3

Kagnew, communication center, 35, 109
Kahsai Berhane, 96
Kalashnikov, 48
Kassebaum, amendment, 25
Katanga, 87, 93, 144
Kay, D., 25

Kellog-Briand Pact, 7, 22
Kelsen, H., 10, 23
Kennedy, J.F., 110
Kenya, 100, 101
Keren, 34
Kessela, 48
Kabra Nagast, 121
Kim, G., 25
King Solomon, 103
Kinnock, N., 153
Kissinger, H., 11, 69, 112
Korean War, 35, 109
Korry, E., 110
Kunz, J., 13, 24

Lachs, P.S., 22
Lancaster House Syndrome, 7
Laissez-Faire, 4
Lansing, R., 57-58
League of Nations, 61
Leland, M., 25
Lenin, V.I., 25, 58
Lewis, A., 162
Libya, 106
Louis Bonaparte, 58

Macedonia, 2
Mahber Shewate, 46
Manichean context of bipolar politics, ?
Marx, K., 22
Marxism-Leninism, guide to Ethiopian policy, 104
Matienzo, A., 37-39, 54, 79, 89
McCloy, J., 132
McNair, Lord, 10, 23
McNamara, R., 131-132, 134
Medicis, 4
Menelik, 81, 103-106
Mengistu, H.M., 105; rise to power of, 113
Meskerem, Journal, 25
Middle East, 99
Military Solution, Dergue's policy of, 120
Modernization, concept of, 110
Mojoryan, 15
Molyneux, M., 121
Monarchy, 3
Morality, origin of, 59

Moose, R., 116
Morocco, 66, 109
Mozambique, 66
Muller, R., 24
Multinational corporations, 14, 15
Mussolini, 106

Namibia, 52, 78, 90
Nasser, G.A., 28, 44
Nationalism, 61
NATO Alliance, 62
Nazi, breach of treaty, trial of leaders, 7
New International Economic Order, 21, 124, 160
Nixon, R.M. 156
Nimeiry, J., relation with Ethiopia and Libya of, 116; regime's instability, 117
Nkrumah, K., 24, 66
Non-alignment, 19; meetings, 68
Non-governmental Organizations (NGOs) and the UN system, 159
Normative order, 74
North-South dialogue, 70, 125
Norway, 31
Nuremberg Trials, 7, 22
Nyerere, J.K., 72

Ogaden, 100, 103; "Ogaden Question"-elements of, 114; Ethiopian repression of, 115; New-Ethiopian offensives in, 116
Operation Bright Star, 116
Organization of African Unity (OAU), 25; first meeting of, 85, 86; charter of, 77; Cairo Resolution of, 114, 146, 151, 154
Organized Labor, 111
Organization of Petroleum Exporting Countries (OPEC), 69, 125, 160
Oromo Liberation Struggle, 107-108

Pacta Sunt Servanda, meaning and application of, 4, 10, 15
Pakistan, 8, 31
Palmerstonian view, 113
Pan-Africanism, 63
Pandora's Box, invocation of, 144
Partition of Eritrea, failed scheme of, 39
Pax Romana, origin of idea, 1
Peaceful coexistence, practice in Africa of, 60
Peace Corps, local involvement of, 111
Peninou, J.L., 121
Peoples Democratic Republic of Ethiopia, 154
Perham, M., 96
Permanent Peoples Tribunal, 82, 86, 87, 90

Persian Gulf, oil from, 99
Philippines, 25, 61, 104
Pinochet, 15
Point Four (USAID), 109
Poland, 30, 58
Positive neutrality, 19
Prebisch, R., 72
Protests, start of in Eritrea, 44, 111

Quebec, 64
Queen of Sheba, legend of, 103

Reagan, R., policies of, 102; aid of, 117
Refugees, from Ogaden, 116
Regionalist Perspective, as opposed to globalist perspective; U.S. foreign policy option of, 99, 100
Religion, origin of, 59
Revision constitution of Ethiopia, 40, 53
Robinson, J., 59, 60
Rodney, W., 125
Roman Law, 3
Roman Oligarchy, 2
Roosevelt, F.D., 23
Rostow, W.W., 67
Rule of Law, 41, 43, 47, 76
Rule, S., 158
Rwelamira, M.R.K., 94

Samir Amin, 72, 125
Schaufele, W., 112
Senghor, L.S., 153
Shoa, Kingdom of, 39
Shurshalov, 23
Singham, A., 72
Somalia, 32, 33, 66, 99, 100, 101, 106, 109; Soviet aid to, 111
South Africa, 15, 17, 31; threat of invasion to, 102
Soviet Jurists, 6
Soviet presence in southern Africa, 112, 117; intervention in the Horn, 101
Soviet Somali Treaty of Friendship, 115
Soviet support of Ethiopia, 117
Soviet Union, 5, 6, 9, 13, 19, 65, 77, 91
Starushenko, 76, 92
Sudan, 46, 48, 109
Sundquist, Amendment of, 25
Sutherland, C.H.V., 21
Syria, 48

Tedla Bairou, 43, 44
Tigray, liberation struggle, 107-108
Tigrigna, 44, 47, 49
Tran-Van-Minh, 56
Trevaskis, K., 34, 49, 51
Trickle down, concept of, 67
Tsegay, Iyassu, 56
Tullock, P., 72
Tunkin, G., 10, 11, 12, 22, 23
Turkish empire, 58

Ucciali, Treaty of, 39
UN Charter, 6, 9, 12, 16, 17, 21, 36, 74-75, 80, 90
UN Commission of Enquiry on Eritrea, 31, 33, 34, 35, 50
UN Conference on Trade and Development, 125, 131
UN General Assembly, resolutions, 8; commission on human rights of Eco-Soc, 27
UN High Commissioner for Refugees, 122
Unionist Party, 34
Universal Declaration of Human Rights, 8-9, 17, 40, 47, 76, 80, 81
USA, 5, 7, 8, 9, 19, 30, 32, 36, 37, 67, 75, 91, 94, 99, 101
US credibility, 112
US economic aid to Ethiopia, 110
US foreign policy, 100
US Freedom of Information Act, 79
US Hopes, on Eritrea/Ethiopia, 117, 118
US Military aid to Ethiopia, 109
US military interest in Ethiopia, 112
US Policy in the Horn of Africa, 109-118
US-Somali relations, 114-116
US strategic interest in the Horn, and problems of regional forces, 118-120

Vance, C., warning to Ethiopia, issued by, 115
Vietnam, 100, 102, 109
Venice, 4
Voice of Eritrea, closing of, 83

War on Want, 121
Warsaw Pact, 11
Weinberger, C., 21
Weiss, P., 25
Wellega, 108
Western-European scholars, role in progress of international law, 4
West Indies, 4
Western Sahara, 25, 78, 90
Weston, B.M., 23
Western Somalia Liberation Front, 115

Wilson, W., 57
Wolde-Ab, W.M., 44-45, 47
Wolpe, H., 22
Woods, G., 131
World Development Report, 132

Yom Kippur, war of, 112
Young, M.C., 93

Zimbabwe, 66